I HEAR YAHWEH

A 30-DAY JOURNEY INTO THE PROPHETIC

CRAIG COONEY

© 2020 by Craig Cooney
Published by DP Publishing
c/o HOPE Church, 20 Highfield Road, Craigavon
Northern Ireland

All rights reserved under International Copyright Law. Contents and/or cover may not be reproduced or transmitted in whole or in part, in any form or by any means, electronic or mechanical, including photocopy, recording or any information storage and retrieval system and without express written consent of the author.

Copyright Notices:
ESV
Scripture taken from the Holy Bible English Standard Version®
Copyright © 2001 by Crossway, a publishing ministry of Good News Publishers. Used by permission. All rights reserved.

NLT
Scripture taken from the Holy Bible New Living Translation®
Copyright © 1996, 2004, 2007, 2013, 2015 by Tyndale House Foundation. Used by permission of Tyndale House Publishers, Inc., Carol Stream, Illinois 60188. All rights reserved.

NIV
Scripture taken from the Holy Bible New International Version® Copyright © 1973, 1978, 1984, 2011 by Biblica Inc. TM
Used by permission of Zondervan. All rights reserved worldwide.

All Scripture references taken from NIV unless otherwise stated.

NKJV
Scripture taken from the New King James Version® Copyright © 1982 by Thomas Nelson. Used by permission. All rights reserved.

Even though the author resides in the UK, he has taken the decision to use Americanized English throughout this book as most of the readers are in the United States. He apologizes to all Anglophiles out there for whom this will be deeply distressing.

CONTENTS

Introduction	1
Day 1: God Is Always Speaking	9
Day 2: It's Your Birthright	18
Day 3: Prophecy and Prophets Today	26
Day 4: Prophetic People and Personalities: Part 1	39
Day 5: Prophetic People and Personalities: Part 2	49
Day 6: How God Speaks: The Bible	62
Day 7: How God Speaks: Impressions	73
Day 8: How God Speaks: The Voices of God	82
Day 9: How God Speaks: Pictures & Visions: Part 1	95
Day 10: How God Speaks: Pictures & Visions: Part 2	106
Day 11: How God Speaks: Dreams: Part 1	116
Day 12: How God Speaks: Dreams: Part 2	134
Day 13: How God Speaks: Dreams: Part 3	148
Day 14: How God Speaks: Words of Knowledge: Part 1	161
Day 15: How God Speaks: Words of Knowledge: Part 2	170

Day 16: How God Speaks: Discernment: Part 1	181
Day 17: How God Speaks: Discernment: Part 2	192
Day 18: How God Speaks: Discernment: Part 3	204
Day 19: How Prophecy Comes Forth	217
Day 20: Prophetic Prayer: Part 1	229
Day 21: Prophetic Prayer: Part 2	240
Day 22: Prophetic Wisdom: Giving Prophetic Words	254
Day 23: Prophetic Wisdom: Receiving Prophetic Words	268
Day 24: Journaling	282
Day 25: The Heart of The Prophetic	296
Day 26: Prophetic Character	307
Day 27: Prophetic Evangelism	320
Day 28: How to Spot A False Prophet	333
Day 29: Stirring Up Your Prophetic Gift	347
Day 30: It's Time to Speak Out	356

INTRODUCTION

We arrived at Ruth's house in a leafy south Dublin suburb at mid-morning. Coffee and tea had already been prepared. After exchanging pleasantries, we moved into the living room, Becky and I sitting on one sofa, Ruth on the other.

We all knew why we were there.

Ruth, along with her husband Matt and two wonderful kids were part of the church we were leading in inner-city Dublin. They had joined around the same time as we had arrived in 2011. They were deeply committed, passionate about God, seeking to please Him in every part of their lives. Ruth and Matt even led worship together in our Sunday gatherings.

But something was wrong.

For over a year Ruth had been bleeding. Like the woman with the issue of blood in Mark 5, doctors and specialists had run test after test but couldn't get to the root of the issue. They were confounded. There was nothing physically wrong with her. Yet, the bleeding wouldn't stop.

Men are generally very uncomfortable talking about these things. However, by this stage of our time ministering in Dublin, I had become pretty unshockable. I'd seen and heard it all.

With tears in her eyes, Ruth described the impact of her condition on her marriage. It affected her ability to be intimate with her husband. She felt self-conscious about it, almost unclean. Plus, she had once been a keen runner. This condition had stopped her from running in over a year.

She was trying to stay strong in her faith and trust God for healing. But after all this time, she was really struggling.

"What happened in April 2009?", I asked her.

Ruth looked at me blankly, somewhat confused as to why I was enquiring about something so long ago. This was now 2014.

"Think back," I said. "Was there anything unusual that happened to you in April 2009?"

Earlier that morning, as we prepared to visit Ruth, I had been praying into her situation. For some reason, the thought entered my mind that I was to ask her about that specific time period. It was just a sense I had, a lingering thought, nothing more. But I had written it down in my journal.

I could see Ruth's mind processing, attempting to pull up memories from the past.

After a few moments, her face looked quite shocked.

"That's when we left our former church," she said. "That was the exact month when we left our church."

I asked her to tell me more.

For years her family had been deeply involved in a church that had been planted by a pastor/missionary from America. In fact, Matt was one of four elders in the church. Their entire lives revolved around services and meetings.

At the start, it had seemed wonderful, with strong Biblical teaching, especially about the End Times. However, as time passed, some things became troubling. The pastor became more and more controlling. If they missed a meeting, they were privately (and sometimes publicly) rebuked. Once, when Ruth needed Matt to stay home because she was unwell, the pastor accused her of being rebellious and leading her husband into compromise.

It reached the stage where almost every decision they made had to be approved by the pastor. He carefully controlled the flock with an increasing mixture of fear, manipulation and guilt. The church came before everything, including family.

By 2009, Matt and Ruth had reached breaking point. As they prayed and prayed about the situation, the Lord began to draw their attention to different things they had overlooked or chosen not to notice: the frequent outbursts of anger from the pastor, the unhappiness and lack of joy among the people, the lack of the Lord's presence in their meetings.

Slowly, their eyes were opened.

In April 2009, Matt resigned from his position as an elder and they left the church.

Within a few weeks, the other three elders had resigned and their families also made an exit. Not long after, the church closed and the pastor returned to the States.

Ruth was stunned that I had asked her about this specific month which was more than five years prior to our meeting.

I pushed a little further: "Did anything unusual happen after you left the church?"

Again I could see Ruth's brain processing, thinking back to that time which she had been trying to forget.

"Yes. I had a miscarriage a few months later," she said. "But here's the strange thing. Every one of the other three elder's wives had miscarriages around the same time."

"Okay," I said. "Here's what I think has happened. I believe the Lord highlighted that date to me because your former pastor placed a curse over your family and the other elders' families when you left the church. You had willingly chosen to fully submit to his authority and that submission was recognized in the spiritual realm. Even though you physically removed yourself from the church, he still had a level of authority over your lives."

(I know some reading this will be shocked that a Christian pastor could or would put a curse over fellow believers. This is a subject for another book entirely, but I have seen it happen more than once, sometimes with horrendous consequences.)

"Here's what we're going to do," I said. "As your pastors, Becky and I now have spiritual authority in your life. That gives us the power the override the previous authority this pastor held over you and speak life and wholeness into your body. I want you to renounce and cancel his authority and we will pray for freedom and healing over your life."

During the next 20 minutes or so, that's exactly what happened. We laid hands on Ruth and spoke deliverance and restoration over her body and her family.

We all felt something shift and left her house just after 12.00 noon.

One hour later she called Becky to say that the bleeding had completely stopped.

That evening she went out for her first run in over a year.

The condition has never returned. She was free.

That is just one of the many reasons why I love the prophetic.

When God whispers to you, it can unlock things that have been bound up for a very long time. God's voice brings life, freedom, wholeness, healing, hope, restoration, direction, purpose, joy, understanding, and so much more.

I have witnessed it again and again.

Here's the thing. Back in 2014, when this situation with Ruth took place, I was just beginning my journey of learning to hear God's voice. While I had regularly encountered the prophetic through other people, I was only starting to grasp that God could speak to me. That He wanted to speak to me. And that I could hear Him.

Since then, God has been growing and developing this area of my life. I have studied Scripture and read many books, listened to seminars and attended conferences, and have been exposed to many prophetic people from various backgrounds.

But, most importantly of all, I have stepped out and taken risks in sharing what I believe God has said to me. This has been in church gatherings, as I personally prophesy over individuals, in ordinary everyday situations as I share a word of encouragement with the barista in the coffee shop or a neighbor in the development where we live, and, more recently, through my ministry online with Daily Prophetic.

Often I have gotten it right. At other times, I've completely missed the mark. But I am committed to growing and developing.

I now want to take you on a journey of learning to hear God's voice for yourself.

You can do it, even if you've never heard Him before. As we will soon see, it's your birthright as a child of God.

Every house needs a solid foundation, so we'll start by exploring what the Bible teaches about the prophetic. The study of Scripture is also crucial to knowing God's ways and His heart for people.

Then we'll look at how your personality and uniqueness affect how you primarily hear God.

We'll explore different aspects of the prophetic such a words, dreams, pictures, visions, impressions, signs and even bodily sensations.

Then we'll take some time to examine how we know it's God and not just our own thoughts (or even the enemy seeking to deceive us.)

We'll think together about how to share prophetic insight with others and avoid some pitfalls which could hinder your effectiveness and hurt others, including what to do when you get it wrong.

Throughout the book there will be practical exercises, from journaling to messaging a friend with an encouraging word.

We'll take time to explore how speaking God's word over your own life, family and future can shape your destiny.

Plus, so much more.

Throughout it all, I will share many stories and illustrations, some my own, some from other people. These will help bring to life the different aspects of hearing God's voice.

So, are you ready?

Let's begin our journey together into the prophetic....

(Note: When sharing personal stories, I will often change the names of the individuals involved to protect their privacy. That's what I've done with the story above. All other details are accurate.)

DAY 1

GOD IS ALWAYS SPEAKING

"It is the nature of God to speak, to communicate His thoughts to others. The whole Bible supports the idea. God is speaking. Not God spoke, but God is speaking. He is by His nature continuously articulate. He fills the world with His speaking Voice."

(A. W. Tozer.)

MY FIRST PROPHETIC ENCOUNTER

It was a warm Friday evening on the north coast of Ireland. I was 16 years old. My best friend Simon and I had just finished our school exams and were staying with some friends at their parent's weekend home. This family spent Monday to Friday in our hometown and then at the weekend they drove 90 minutes to be by the sea. That didn't make a lot of sense to me. Apparently, it was because they had discovered a particular church in that area which they loved. My friend Ruth described it as a "charismatic" church.

At this stage, I had been a Christian for a little under two years. Having been raised in a traditional Anglican/Episcopalian church, I'd never heard of the term 'charismatic'. I thought it sounded like a type of washing machine. But here we were, on a Friday evening in May 1992, gathered with over one hundred expectant people of all ages, in a building that looked more like a warehouse than a church to me.

When the worship started, the place erupted. Not only were the congregation singing way too enthusiastically for my liking, but most of the people were dancing. In church! I'd never seen such a thing. Was this even legal?

I tried to join in as best I could, not knowing most of the songs. As for the dancing, I left that to the 'professionals'.

After around 45 minutes, a man who I later found out was the Senior Pastor, stepped up to the microphone. A hush descended over the auditorium. He began to speak in a loud, authoritative tone: "Thus saith the Lord, I am coming to dwell amongst thee. Thou art my sheep and I am thine Shepherd, saith the Lord…."

The people around me became more and more excited as he continued, clapping enthusiastically and shouting 'Amen' and 'Hallelujah'.

I can't remember exactly what else he said that night. At the time I was more than a little confused. What was happening? Who was he speaking to? Why was he using funny language?

Later I found out that he was 'prophesying'. Apparently, God was speaking through this man of God to the people. Even as a young

Christian, I'd read enough of the Bible to know about prophets in the Old Testament and even the gift of prophecy mentioned by the Apostle Paul.

But did God still speak today? And, if so, why did He speak in old King James English?

That weekend left me with many questions. But those few days also changed my life. Later, on that Friday evening, the pastor had laid hands on me and prayed that I would be baptized in the Holy Spirit. It took a while, but slowly and gradually, strange words started coming out of my mouth. I was speaking in sounds and syllables that didn't make sense to me. I was informed that this was 'speaking in tongues'. Again, like prophecy, I had read about this in the Bible. Now I was experiencing it for myself.

On the following Sunday afternoon, as we drove home, I genuinely felt as if I had entered into a whole new spiritual reality. I had experienced a sense of God's presence that I hadn't known even existed.

That first experience of hearing prophecy was almost 30 years ago. However, something was ignited in my heart that evening that has never left me. I became fascinated with the notion that people today could actually hear God speak to them.

Yes, I was put off a little by the 16th century English language.

But still, if God was still speaking today, was it even remotely possible that I could hear Him?

GOD IS NOT SILENT

As I began to study the Bible with fresh eyes, I discovered something: God is incredibly talkative. In the very first chapter of Genesis, we read over and over again: "And God said, let there be….."

The entire creation and cosmos were formed by the voice of God.

Then He began to populate the planet and created the first humans, Adam and Eve, in His own image and likeness (Gen 1: 27). He actually breathed Himself into them. They were carriers of the Divine nature, flesh and bone containers of His holy presence.

Immediately we read, "God blessed them and said to them…" (Gen 1: 28). So, men and women were created with the ability to hear and understand God speaking to them. And they could also talk to Him. They chatted and conversed together. It was all completely normal and natural, just like breathing or walking.

But then they chose to listen to another voice in the Garden. A malevolent, destructive voice. They engaged with the serpent as He contradicted the voice of God and persuaded them to disobey the one explicit prohibition that God had given them. They ate from the tree, giving the voice of the devil authority over their lives.

Immediately they knew something was wrong. Inside, they felt it. It was like something was broken. Twisted and damaged. And they didn't know how to fix it.

Instead of running to God, they hid from Him. They were afraid. It was an emotion they had never known or experienced before. But it was very real.

God found them. Asked them why they were hiding from Him. They attempted to make excuses. Shift the blame.

But the damage could not be undone. We read this: "So the LORD God banished him from the Garden of Eden…." (Gen 3: 23).

God evicted them from His pure, holy presence. Holy and unholy couldn't dwell together. Divinity and humanity were separated. They no longer had unrestricted access to their Creator. And the further they moved away from Him, the more faint and quiet His voice became.

At that point, God could have written humans off completely. We had rebelled against our Maker and so He had every right to cut us off forever. But He chose not to do that. Why not? Simply because of His immense, intense passionate love for us.

He had a plan. He was going to somehow bring us back to where we began – enjoying His presence, hearing His voice. Or to put it more simply, dad was going to do whatever it took to get his kids back home.

It wasn't going to be simple. Nor would it be quick. But nothing would stop Him.

It began with God speaking to an old man named Abram (later to become Abraham). He was called to father a nation, a people who would be God's special possession. He moved as God directed him.

Later, Abraham's great-grandson Joseph had prophetic dreams. This eventually brought God's people to the land of Egypt.

As the years passed, they become enslaved in Egypt. God wanted them to occupy a land of their own, the place He promised to Abraham. So, He spoke through a burning bush to Moses. He revealed Himself as Yahweh, 'I AM', and called on Moses to deliver His people from oppression and lead them towards the Promised Land.

As they sojourned, God continued to speak to and through Moses. They had a very special relationship: "The LORD would speak to Moses face to face, as one speaks to a friend." (Ex 33: 11) Yahweh also gave His people the Law and the Ten Commandments, a written code for them to live by if they were to flourish and thrive in the land He is bringing them into.

After Moses' death, God spoke to Joshua. He would be the one who will lead the people across the Jordan into the land of Canaan.

However, once they arrived there, God's people rebelled against Him, turning to idolatry and immorality.

Yet, still, He continued to speak.

To Gideon through an angel and using a fleece. To Samuel, first as a young boy and then as a seasoned prophet. To King David, directly and through the prophet Nathan.

For centuries God spoke to and through prophets such as Elijah, Isaiah, Jeremiah, and Ezekiel, communicating with words but also through visions, dreams, angels, nature, prophetic acts, inner impressions, a still small voice.

The prophets spoke into their own particular time and circumstances. But they also began to declare that God's deliverer, the Messiah was coming. They are shown many details such as how and where he would be born, the kind of life he would live, and how he would die.

Then, one day, an angel showed up to a teenage girl named Mary. She was preparing to marry Joseph, a decent, hard-working man. The angel informed her that she was pregnant. However, this would be no ordinary child. She was carrying God's son and was to name him Jesus.

This little baby was 'the Word'. God in the flesh. The fullest representation of His being and nature (Heb 1: 1-3).

When Jesus spoke, it was God speaking. His words carried absolute authority.

Demons had to flee at his word.

Storms were stilled at his word.

Blind eyes were opened at his word.

Broken bodies were healed at his word.

The dead were raised to life at his word.

EDEN RESTORED

Jesus was God's Son, the Messiah, the promised deliverer. He had come to complete God's mission and plan to bring His children home. To restore us back into the relationship with the Father that we were created to enjoy. To live in His presence. To hear His voice.

Through his perfect life, his sacrificial death, and his glorious resurrection, Jesus fully and completely accomplished everything the Father asked him to do.

The curtain was torn, the barrier was removed, once and for all.

Access has been restored.

Through faith in Jesus, we are born again. We become children of God. Sons and daughters of the Most High. We are declared righteous and holy before God. We can dwell in His presence again.

A new covenant, or way for people to relate to God, had been initiated. It wasn't through keeping the law or sacrifices or religious rituals. It was through the blood of Jesus.

And, as we'll see tomorrow, that entitles every single one of us to hear His voice. It is our birthright as children of God.

Today, I wanted you to see that we serve a God who speaks. He has never stopped speaking to His people.

At times, it may only have been to select individuals at specific moments.

But our God speaks.

It is His nature to communicate.

And as men and women created in His image and likeness, and born again by His Holy Spirit, we have been given the ability to communicate with Him. To talk to Him and to hear His voice.

It's not just for the chosen few.

It's for you.

Practical Exercise: As you read the Bible in the weeks ahead, take care to note the various ways God speaks to individuals. See how creative and unrestricted He is as He communicates to and through His people.

DAY 2

IT'S YOUR BIRTHRIGHT

"Each of us was created with a deep inner longing to hear our Master's voice. He didn't make us to be mechanical robots that just march around doing preordained things. It is our birthright to have an actual relationship with our God."

(James Goll)

I have an old Bible in my study. It contains five pages filled with handwritten prophetic words that I received between 1992-1994. These were the two years immediately following the experience that I described in the previous chapter when I encountered prophecy for the first time and was filled with the Holy Spirit. It seemed as if the floodgates had been opened. Once I realized and accepted that God still communicated with his children today, He began to speak to me with increased regularity through pastors, prophets, missionaries, and even my high school economics teacher!

Many of these words were remarkably similar. I was called to leadership. I would preach His Word. God was preparing me. They set my life on a clear trajectory and sustained me through the next decade.

However, these were always words given through other people. I considered most of them to be special individuals, maybe even super-spiritual. They must have a special gift of prophecy, I reasoned.

I still couldn't fathom that God could actually speak directly to me or through me to others.

THE PROMISE OF THE PROPHETIC

Yesterday we saw that the Old Testament prophets often spoke of the coming Messiah, the one who would deliver God's people. When Jesus arrived, He clearly fulfilled those predictions.

However, the prophets also envisioned a day when the Holy Spirit would not be confined to being poured out upon a few particular individuals for specific tasks. A time was coming when the Spirit would be poured out without limit or measure upon *all* of God's people.

For example, Ezekiel foresaw a time when the Holy Spirit would indwell the people of God and move them to obedience:

"I will give you a new heart and put a new spirit in you; I will remove from you your heart of stone and give you a heart of flesh. And I will put my Spirit in you and move you to follow my decrees and be careful to keep my laws." (Ez 36: 26-27)

Then later, the prophet Joel took this promise from God a step further:

"I will pour out my Spirit on all people.
Your sons and daughters will prophesy,
your old men will dream dreams,
your young men will see visions.
Even on my servants, both men and women,
I will pour out my Spirit in those days."

(Joel 2: 28-29)

Think about what you just read. God said He would pour out His Holy Spirit upon ALL people. Not only Jews. Not just a select few. Not only those who pray for three hours each morning. Not just those with a unique gift.

ALL people. That includes you.

What would the result be?

Men and women, young and old, would one day prophesy and experience supernatural dreams and visions.

God does not discriminate. This will be available to everyone.

This promise of the Spirit's outpouring was clearly fulfilled on the day of Pentecost. This is the era we are living in. The age of the Spirit.

It should be abnormal *not* to hear God's voice with regularity.

If God's Spirit lives inside you, you can hear Him speak.

Jesus himself made that abundantly clear. In describing himself as the Good Shepherd, look at what he says:

"The sheep hear his voice, and he calls his own sheep by name and leads them out. When he has brought out all his own, he goes before them, and the sheep follow him, for they know his voice." (John 10: 3-4)

The sheep *hear* his voice.

The sheep *know* his voice.

What Jesus is saying is that it is the birthright of every single believer to hear and understand the voice of God.

No exceptions. No exclusions.

If you are a Christian, born again of the Spirit, you can hear God's voice.

It is not so much a matter of giftedness as it is of relationship.

TUNING INTO GOD'S THOUGHTS

Our family has just returned from a vacation by the sea. I love the beach. How soft the sand feels as it scrunches between my toes. Walking on the shoreline as the waves wash over my feet. Climbing the steep sand dunes and then rolling down them with my little son.

In Psalm 139, David says this:

"How precious to me are your thoughts concerning me, God!
How vast is the sum of them!
Were I to count them,
they would outnumber the grains of sand."

Think about that. Imagine scooping up one handful of sand. Could you count the single grains? It would be impossible. The Bible says that the thoughts God has about you outnumber all of the grains of sand on the earth. That includes beaches, deserts and golf course bunkers!

There is never a moment when God is not thinking about His children.

In its most basic form then, prophecy is simply picking up on God's thoughts. It's tuning into the chatter of Heaven. It's hearing and communicating the heart of the Father towards His children and His creation.

Right now, all around you, are sound waves. You can't see them or hear them. But they are very real. You simply need a radio to tune into them.

So too it is with God's voice. He is always speaking in so many different and various ways. The problem is simply that we aren't tuned into Him. We're too busy. Our lives are too noisy. Or we don't expect to hear His voice therefore we aren't listening.

Or perhaps we simply don't know how to tune in.

That's what we're going to move onto in the coming days.

We're going to get very practical on how you can hear, recognize, and understand God's voice for yourself.

First, let me dispel the notion that you have to reach a certain level of maturity and spirituality before God will speak to you.

DAD'S TALK TO THEIR BABIES

I remember so clearly the exact moment our son Elijah was born. It was 9.01 am on Sunday 16th September 2012. It had been a long and painful labor for Becky. She had been rushed to the emergency theatre and I had been absolutely terrified. Of losing the baby. Of losing my wife.

The consultant doctor told me not to worry if the baby didn't make any noises when he came out. That stressed me even more. What was wrong with my child?

In the end, Elijah Fletcher Cooney emerged as a very healthy 8lb 4oz screaming bundle of flesh. From the moment he was placed into my arms, I felt a love for him I had never known before. I knew I would literally do anything to take care of this boy.

From that moment, I also talked to him. A lot. I told him how much I loved him. How proud I was of him. Of how handsome he was.

Of course, he couldn't understand a single word I said. But that didn't matter. I just wanted him to hear his daddy's voice. And I knew that if I kept talking, a day would come soon when he would begin to recognize the words and communicate back to me.

I believe it's similar in our relationship with God. You are His beloved child. He is your doting Dad. Therefore, He is talking to you. He's not waiting until you have been a believer for 6 years or 60 years or have attained a certain degree of spiritual maturity or theological knowledge before He speaks to you. He's expressing His heart over you right now. He declaring His desires for your future. He's whispering about your friends and family members. He's showing you what lies ahead.

Maybe you can't understand Him yet, at least not fully.

That's okay. He's not going to stop talking.

Gradually, over the coming weeks and months, you will learn the language of Heaven. You'll tune into the frequency of the Father's voice. You'll start to notice things which have always been there, in a new way. You will begin to heed the subtle nudges and trust the inner voice.

In the next chapter, we'll look at what the New Testament says about the purpose of prophecy and jump into some really practical ways that you can start to develop and grow in your ability to hear God's voice today.

Practical Exercise: Has God spoken to you in the past? Perhaps directly or through other people? Did you write these words down? If so, find them and re-read them. Remind yourself of what God has said. Consider if any of them have been fulfilled in your life so far. Perhaps pray into those that have yet to be fulfilled.

DAY 3

PROPHECY AND PROPHETS TODAY

"The goal of revelation is so simple: See what God sees, hear what God hears, and speak what God speaks so we can all love the way God loves. Revelation is given to us so we can carry a piece of God's heart from eternity into the world."

(Shawn Bolz)

I had just fumbled and floundered my way through a message in front of 120 of my fellow high school students at Scripture Union. Scripture Union (or SU) is a bit like Campus Crusade, but for younger students. Even in our public school of 700 students, around one in every five teenagers attended the SU. The weekly gatherings basically consisted of a time of worship followed by a relevant message.

Even though I had only been a believer for around three years, I was on the small leadership team that organized the meetings and booked guest speakers. A few days before this we had received a call to say that our scheduled speaker for that week would be unable to make it for some reason. What were we going to do? We'd never be able to find a replacement at such short notice.

After a long and protracted silence, I uttered the words, "I'll speak."

The other four members of the team looked at me with a mixture of surprise and relief. It wasn't that I had never spoken before. Even at the age of just 17, I had already been sensing some sort of call to ministry and had spoken three or four times at various youth events. The difference then was that I always had weeks to prepare. Now, I only had a few days. But somehow inside I sensed that I needed to step up.

I can't even recall what I spoke about that day. But what I do vividly remember is the feeling that I had made a total mess of it. My nerves had gotten the better of me. My hands had shaken constantly. I'd lost my place a number of times. I kept stuttering and repeating myself. And then I attempted to use really bad humor to cover up my rising feelings of embarrassment and humiliation.

In hindsight, it probably wasn't as awful as I imagined, but as I sat down and we sang the final song, I had one thought in my mind: I never, ever want to do that ever again. Whatever God had in my future, it wasn't going to be speaking.

After the meeting, everyone quickly went on their way. I stayed behind, stacking chairs and tidying the room. Also, I was hoping to avoid talking to anyone about the car crash of a message that they had just witnessed.

"Craig, can I have a chat with you?", said a voice from behind me.

I turned and saw Mr. Grant, the economics teacher standing there.

'Uh-oh', I thought. It must have been really bad.

I followed the teacher into his classroom and stood there expecting the worst.

"Craig, as I watched you up there today, I felt God speak to me about you", he began. "I believe God wants me to tell you that He has called you to preach His Word. He has especially anointed you to communicate His heart to others. But, to prepare, you must immerse yourself in the Scriptures. God has incredible plans and purposes for your life. I just wanted to share that with you. Okay Craig, see you tomorrow."

Trying to hold back the tears that were streaming down my face, I left the classroom.

I don't think Mr. Grant will ever know just how much those 45 seconds of prophetic encouragement that day altered my life.

IT'S NOT ABOUT ME...

At its core, the prophetic is not about ecstatic experiences or booming voices from Heaven or otherworldly visions. **The prophetic is about encouragement.**

Prophecy is also distinct from simply hearing God's voice for yourself. We have already seen how every believer can hear the Father. It's your birthright as a child of God.

Prophecy, on the other hand, *is when you hear God's voice for someone else.* It could be a friend, a group of people, a church, a community, a company, even a nation. **The focus is always on expressing the heart, mind, will and intentions of God for other people.**

Paul made this clear in 1 Corinthians 14 when he wrote to a church that was a little overenthusiastic about dramatic spiritual experiences:

"...the one who prophesies speaks to people for their strengthening, encouraging and comfort."

The primary purpose of the prophetic is not to expose sin or foretell the future; it is to strengthen, encourage and comfort others. Other translations use the words 'edification, exhortation and consolation'.

What do each of these words mean?

Edification simply means to build up. A true prophetic word serves to build up one's faith, confirm their calling and strengthen their relationship with God. It should draw them closer to Jesus and other believers. It calls out the treasure hidden inside the jar of clay (2 Corinthians 4: 7).

Exhortation is a word for stirring things up. It encourages people to persevere and to not give up on their promises to God in hard times, and to not give in to discouragement or sin. It should embolden and bring fresh hope and courage to the life of the believer or church.

Consolation means to bring the type of comfort that helps ease feelings of grief, loss or pain. Life can be very difficult for many people. Hearts get shattered and dreams can be crushed. Consolation may not make the pain go away. But it can bring fresh hope and help them to see God's perspective in the midst of their disappointment or setback.

When people ask me how they can begin to develop their prophetic gifting, my answer is always the same – **everywhere you go, begin to look around for individuals who might need some encouragement.** At the supermarket checkout, when chatting with your neighbor, when waiting at the school gate with other parents - simply start to speak words of life, hope, faith, courage, blessing and positivity. I promise, you'll be amazed at the impact it will have.

Many people have no idea just how much God loves them. Others have become bogged down with guilt, regrets, discouragement and the demands of life.

At its essence, the prophetic reminds them of who they truly are. It reveals how God perceives them. That they are seen, loved and special. They were created with purpose and destiny.

The prophetic simply brings out the best in people. That is what Mr. Grant did for a 17-year-old high school student. And almost 30 years on, I've never forgotten his words. He had no idea at the time, but that short conversation marked me for life.

Just think, you could have that impact on someone today.

Of course, there are many other elements to the prophetic. We'll explore those in more detail as we go through this journey together.

THE DIFFERENCES BETWEEN OLD TESTAMENT AND NEW TESTAMENT PROPHECY

Right now, I'm sure some of you are thinking, 'Craig, that doesn't sound much like the prophets in the Bible. Jeremiah and Ezekiel didn't go around telling God's people how great they were'.

I would absolutely agree. And there is a time for rebuke, correction and direction in the prophetic.

But first, unless we truly grasp that God's heart is *for* people, not against them, we will never be effective at sharing what God is saying.

God never changes. However, *the covenant or agreement through which He relates to humanity has changed.*

It is crucial to understand this. Old Testament prophets related to God through an Old Covenant paradigm. They were unique individuals who were anointed by the Holy Spirit to be God's spokesmen (or women) for a particular era.

Old Testament prophets saw the world through the lens of the law of God which had been broken again and again. Thus, they boldly denounced sin, pronounced judgements, issued warnings, foretold the future, and called the people back to Yahweh.

They often represented Yahweh in the presence of kings and were expected to speak the perfect, inspired words of God. There was no margin for error. One mistake and they could be condemned as being false prophets and might even be stoned to death (Deuteronomy 18: 20).

Many of the prophet's words were recorded for us and are part of the Bible. That's why we have the books of Isaiah, Jeremiah, Ezekiel, Amos, and so on. To disobey the prophet was to disobey God Himself and would often lead to punishment or disaster.

After the final Old Testament prophet Malachi spoke, there was a period of silence for around 400 years. It was as if God was closing the door on one era, while a new one was opened.

Then Jesus entered our world. *And through Christ's life, death and resurrection, everything has changed.*

Jesus totally fulfilled God's law through his perfect obedience. He never once sinned. He took our place and paid for our punishment. God's wrath and judgement for sin were poured upon him. Justice has been served. Mercy is now available.

We now live under a completely new covenant or agreement between God and humanity. The Old Testament Law no longer defines the way in which we connect to God or God relates to us. The Holy Spirit has been poured out on all believers, not just a few chosen men and women.

Of course, there will one day be a final judgement for the unrepentant. Scripture makes that very clear. But, presently, we are living in the era of grace.

New Testament prophecy, therefore now sees each person, not through the law or sin, but through the lens of Jesus' shed blood.

That changes everything.

Instead of pointing out where people fall short, we remind them of who they really are in Christ. Rather than highlighting sin and failure, we call them back to their true identity. Prophetic people are no longer the lone voice for God declaring His word into a situation. We are part of a loving community of faith, seeking His face together and building one another up.

At times we may need to challenge unrighteousness, speak up for truth and highlight injustice. But *it is always with a redemptive filter*, emphasizing on the possibility of genuine transformation through Christ.

IF I PROPESY, AM I A PROPHET?

This question causes much confusion among believers. Are there still prophets today, and if so, what makes someone a prophet?

The New Testament makes it clear that God has called certain people to the function or office of prophet in the church. For example, Ephesians 4: 11-12 says:

"Christ himself gave the apostles, the **prophets**, the evangelists, the pastors and teachers, to equip his people for works of service, so that the body of Christ may be built up."

In Acts 11: 27 we also read:

"During this time some **prophets** came down from Jerusalem to Antioch."

And Acts 15: 32 says:

"Judas and Silas, who themselves were **prophets**, said much to encourage and strengthen the believers."

So, it seems clear that the role of prophet exists within the Christian church. They were, and are, foundational to the life of the Body of Christ and exist to develop, equip and release believers into their calling and destiny.

However, the office or role of a prophet is different and distinct from the ability of a believer to prophesy or hear God's voice.

When we receive Jesus as our Lord and Saviour through repentance and faith, the Holy Spirit comes and lives inside us. With the gift of the Spirit, every believer has the ability to manifest or demonstrate the Spirit in nine clear and distinct ways. These are outlined in 1 Corinthians 12: 7-11:

"Now to each one the manifestation of the Spirit is given for the common good. To one there is given through the Spirit a message of wisdom, to another a message of knowledge by means of the same Spirit, to another faith by the same Spirit, to another gifts of healing by that one Spirit, to another miraculous powers, **to another prophecy**, to another distinguishing between spirits, to another speaking in different kinds of tongues, and to still another the interpretation of tongues. All these are the work of one and the same Spirit, and he distributes them to each one, just as he determines."

These gifts are diffused and distributed throughout the body of Christ. While some people think that each Christian has one or two gifts, I believe that every Christian can manifest each of these nine gifts at different times as the Spirit enables them. In other words, all believers have the potential to see people healed when they pray or to bring a word of wisdom or knowledge as they exercise their faith in certain situations.

One of these manifestations is prophecy. Again, all believers have the ability to hear God speak and to bring forth a prophetic message to another person or people as the situation requires it.

Does that make them a prophet?

No.

There is a difference between the spiritual gift of prophecy and the office of a prophet.

Those who are called to the office of a prophet are men and women who, over time, have demonstrated the ability to bring forth the word of the Lord with significantly increased clarity, accuracy and frequency than other people. Their gift and function are recognized by church leadership. Prophets don't label themselves by that title so much as it is conferred upon them by those in positions of spiritual authority.

Also, some people seem naturally more prophetic than others, in the same way as some people are more pastoral or compassionate than others. They are more spiritually sensitive and find it easier to sense what God is saying. We'll explore that more in the next chapter.

It's also entirely possible for someone to mature and develop in their prophetic gifting over time to such a degree that they begin to be accepted by church leaders and other believers as a prophet. They have built up a history of credibility and trust through the accuracy of their words and their ability to discern the will of the Lord.

For example, I am not a prophet, nor have I ever called myself a prophet. I am someone, however, who has a prophetic gifting that I am constantly seeking to grow and develop. Consequently, the frequency and accuracy of my prophetic words have increased in recent years as I have learned to recognize God's voice with greater clarity and have taken more risks in sharing what I believe He is saying. There may come a time in the future when I step into the office of a prophet. Or it may never happen. Either way, I am simply seeking to be obedient to Scripture which admonishes believers to "eagerly desire gifts of the Spirit, especially prophecy." (1 Corinthians 14: 1)

There is so much more we could go into regarding the roles of prophets in the Old and New Testaments. This chapter could be an entire book in itself. However, my goal here has been to give you an overview of the different ways the prophetic operates today so that you are able to distinguish between:

(i) Old Testament and New Testament prophecy; and,

(ii) Hearing God's voice for yourself versus hearing it for other people.

Now, let's move on to discuss the characteristics of prophetic people and the different prophetic personalities which influence how you hear God's voice.

PRACTICAL EXERCISE: Throughout your day, actively seek out opportunities to encourage other people. Notice them. Compliment them. Have real conversations. Lift them up. Ask God to help you see each person through His eyes.

DAY 4

PROPHETIC PEOPLE AND PERSONALITIES:

PART 1

"Whether your experiences were God-ordained or not, He wants to use everything in your life as an opportunity to hear His voice, see His face, and engage with His heart. You've studied what you've studied because God wants to use you in that area. He wants you to access that knowledge as He uses you to impact the world around you. God wants to use your experience in life."

(Julian Adams)

The well-known and respected prophet had been teaching the room of around 100 people for most of the day. While the instruction was great, if I'm being honest, I mostly wanted to watch him in action. Even more than that, I was hoping for a clear and directive word relating to my life, our family and what the future might hold.

He started to pick people out of the crowd and prophesy over them. I could tell by their expressions that he was nailing it each time. Then, towards the end of the session, he looked directly at Becky and me. "Here we go," I thought. My heart began to beat a little faster.

The prophet began to open his mouth.

But then he suddenly stopped as if interrupted by something or someone.

He immediately shifted his gaze to a middle-aged man sitting on the other side of the room and asked him to stand.

What was going on? A little like Jesus getting interrupted by the woman with the bleeding condition on his way to heal Jairus' daughter, I couldn't help but feel like this other man had 'stolen' my prophetic word!

The prophet began to speak to the man about his childhood and how he'd never known the affection of a father.

The middle-aged man was expressionless.

The prophet went on to tell him about how he had built up walls in his heart, determined never to show emotion or allow anyone in.

The recipient appeared totally unmoved.

As the words continued to flow from his mouth, the prophet stepped forward. He stood directly in front of the man, put his arms around him and gave him a hug.

'That's nice,' I thought. 'Now maybe you can come back to us.'

But the prophet didn't move. Nor did he speak. He simply stood there embracing this total stranger in front of us all.

The middle-aged man appeared somewhat uncomfortable.

The prophet didn't let him go.

Soon I was feeling uncomfortable. This was getting awkward.

For what seemed like an hour but in actuality was around five minutes, these two men stood there, one embracing the other.

Then the recipient of the word began to shake and cry. At first gently, then sobbing uncontrollably. The prophet continued to silently hold him in his arms. The man was convulsing now, heaves and deep groans rising up from his innermost being.

The prophet was getting soaked with the man's tears. But he still held him tightly.

For 10 to 15 minutes, that was all he did - hold him - as decades of pain were released.

Then, the meeting was over.

This all happened 7 years ago. While I still think it would have been nice to receive a prophetic word that day, I was incredibly moved, even marked, by what I had witnessed.

This prophet hadn't merely spoken the word of the Lord. He had fully embodied it, physically expressing the very heart and emotions of God. Words would never have been enough to penetrate this wounded soul, hardened by years of rejection and pain. He needed to experience the loving embrace of the Father.

YOU HAVE A UNIQUE PERSONALITY AND HISTORY

Each of us is totally different. The place where we were born, the family in which we were raised, the events of our childhood and adolescence, and relationships we have developed, and the multitude of experiences, good and bad, that we have had on our journey up until this moment, have all profoundly shaped us.

Who you are today is a combination of your genetics and your history. This also includes your spiritual history.

You are not exactly like any other human on the planet.

Therefore, how you hear from God and how you share His heart with others will not be like anyone else. The Father will speak to you in a different and distinct way than He speaks to anyone else.

Do you remember what Jesus said in John 10?

"… the sheep listen to his voice. He calls his own sheep by name and leads them out….I am the good shepherd; I know my sheep and my sheep know me." (vv. 3; 14)

God knows your name and speaks to you individually.

This means that you might not hear God like everyone else hears Him. That's completely okay. You do you. Be a voice, not an echo or clone of someone else.

CHARACTERISTICS OF PROPHETIC PEOPLE

While every believer can hear the voice of God, I have noticed over the years that particular people, by personality, nature and temperament, seem to find it easier than others. They just tend to be a little more spiritually sensitive than most people.

R. Loren Sandford, in his excellent book *Understanding Prophetic People*, says this:

"Prophetic people vary in nature as widely as the population in general, while sharing to a significant degree a number of personality elements and life experiences. We come in all sizes and shapes, some of us serious in nature and some of us loving a good joke, some intellectual and others having no education at all. But at heart, we are much alike in many respects."

While the following list is by no means comprehensive or definitive, here are some of my own observations about people who are more naturally prophetic than others.

Prophetic people:

- Have a strong sense of being drawn towards the prophetic and/or intercessory prayer.
- Will often 'just know' what is about to happen before it occurs.
- Often say things like: "I don't know what it is, but there is just something 'off' about that person."
- Look at people and see things that aren't visible in the natural.
- Discern deception and lies before others see it.
- Sense the atmosphere changing in the room before anyone else does.
- Are very conscious that there is an invisible/spiritual realm influencing and impacting the world around them.
- Often feel things in their 'gut' about people, situations and places.
- Will feel the 'weight' of a situation much more than most people.
- Will be deeply burdened to pray while everyone thinks everything is fine.

- Become grieved when the Holy Spirit is grieved.

- Will have 'random' people and places come into their mind as the Spirit prompts them to intercede and pray.

- Can't tolerate things that other people readily accept.

- Can often come across as too direct or blunt because they see things as being black and white. They tend to make quick judgements about what they see and hear.

- Feel deep righteous anger when they witness injustice and oppression.

- Tend to need more time away from the noise and busyness of life than other people.

- Enjoy deep friendships but get drained quickly by crowds and superficial conversations.

- Experience deep conviction when they permit impurity or sin to have access into their life.

- Feel empty and barren more quickly when they neglect to spend time in God's presence.

- Feel 'homesick' when they haven't spent time with the Father.

- Are frustrated by a lukewarm-ness and a lack of spiritual passion in others.
- Can be very impatient when change happens slower than they think it should.
- Tend to be more focused on the future than the past or even the present.
- Notice small things that most people miss.
- See patterns and signs in numbers, symbols and everyday events more than most people.
- Have a strong ability to empathize and sense others' pain.
- Can often feel misunderstood and that they don't really fit in.
- Can appear to be more 'intense' than other people.
- Are loyal to truth even if it means cutting off some relationships.
- May struggle to really settle or feel 'at home' because you are ready to move wherever the Spirit leads.
- Struggle to be satisfied spiritually because they know there is so much more of God and the Kingdom that they have yet to see and experience.

- Often struggle with deep sleep as their dream life is very active and vivid.

- Will often experience extreme resistance from the enemy in places where he has had a stronghold for a long time.

Did you find yourself nodding in agreement with many of the above statements? If so, you are already hearing God speak much more than you probably realized.

If you didn't, don't worry. You can train, develop and attune your senses to become more aware of how the Father is communicating with you.

Being a prophetic person can be a huge blessing. You get to see and sense what God is doing and get to express His heart to others. However, it can also have some significant downsides. Julian Adams, a seasoned and respected prophet originally from South Africa, has written the following from his own first-hand experience. I personally have found his insights incredibly helpful.

"You will often find that prophetic people have lived through seasons of extreme rejection. This might not be true for everyone, but it is my experience that prophetic people will often go through hardships and rejection that will drive them into deeper intimacy

with God. This is often why prophetic people are misunderstood to be shy, introverted and seriously insecure!

The reason I put this in here is that very seldom do you find a confident prophet. Most prophetic people will live with a sense of insecurity and a lack of confidence. You will see this clearly as you watch the life of an emerging prophetic person.

Prophetic people will often seem to have "foot-in-mouth" disease. They will often say things without realising what they are saying and will put their foot in it. They can touch on something that has been an issue and then pass their opinion (or sometimes God's wisdom) on it without even realising it. Sometimes it will seem as if they come across as intense and very black and white. This is not to be misunderstood as sharpness or being too direct, it just seems to be the way prophets work."

The blessings and burdens of being a prophetic person often go hand in hand. You will often feel things that you struggle to articulate. At times, it can be a lonely road. You may be misunderstood and rejected, even within the church. But you can't deny it. You just 'know' that some things are true and 'sense' that some things will happen.

How do you 'know' and 'sense' these things?

That is what we'll explore in the next chapter as we continue to look at different aspects and characteristics of your prophetic personality.

DAY 5

PROPHETIC PEOPLE AND PERSONALITIES:

PART 2

"You are an original. While it is important to learn from and be inspired by others, don't ever be a copy or a clone. God doesn't want to just communicate through any voice. He wants to speak through YOUR voice. He longs to express all that He is through all that you are."

(Craig Cooney)

One morning in late May 2018, I kneeled on the floor in my study with a pen in my hand and a blank page on the chair before me. I simply said the following words: "Father, what do you want to say to your people?"

After a few minutes, a single word came into my mind. I wrote it down. Then a few more thoughts followed, related to that initial word.

A little while later, I assembled my scribbles into something coherent and typed them onto a little white square using an app on my phone. Somewhat nervously, I posted them on an Instagram account that I had registered just the day before. I had deliberated over various names. In the end, I chose the name @Daily.Prophetic.

Honestly, I mostly just wanted to learn how to use this new social media platform. Before this, I had only been active on Facebook but had started to hear everyone talk about Instagram. I figured a few people might follow the page and be encouraged. Plus, having studied marketing at university, it was always good to keep up with what the 'kids' were using. That was as much as I hoped for.

The following day, I repeated the process. And then the next. And so on.

Amazingly, some people actually started to follow my page. As I kept posting, the numbers grew at a rate I could never have anticipated.

Some days a word would come to mind. Other days, I would notice something – a tree without leaves, a road sign, a line in a sermon, my little boy playing, lyrics from a song. Occasionally God would give me a short vision or picture. At other times, I felt something bubble up inside me, so I pressed record on my phone and started speaking it out into a dictation app.

Week after week, I simply kept posting what I heard, saw, or sensed.

And, somehow, the number of followers kept growing.

As I write this, it's been just over two years ago since Daily Prophetic started. Honestly, I'm just as stunned and humbled today as I was back then.

None of this was planned. There was no strategy. There still isn't.

My process hasn't changed. I still write every new post the exact same way. I simply try to hear what God is saying and I share it.

HOW DO YOU PRIMARILY HEAR FROM GOD?

In the previous chapter, we began to explore prophetic personalities. You are uniquely designed by God and no one else on the planet has had the exact same background and life experiences as you. Therefore, how the Father communicates with you will be specifically tailored to your personality. Of course, you will have commonalities with other people. But your prophetic expression will flow through the filter of your distinct individuality.

In this chapter, we will look at two different facets of your prophetic personality that will shape how you hear from God and then how you process what you hear. I have called these *forms* and *filters*.

FORMS: HOW GOD SPEAKS

While we all hear God differently, there are four primary ways that people tend to receive prophetic revelation: ***knowing, hearing, feeling and seeing.***

Let's explore each of them.

KNOWERS just 'know' in their mind or 'gut' that something is true and right. They are highly intuitive. They can't really explain how they 'know' - they just do. Knowers will frequently have 'a-ha' or lightbulb moments when something just clicks or suddenly makes sense.

My wife is a 'knower'. While I like to think that I'm fairly intuitive, Becky definitely 'picks up' on things before I do. She can walk into a room of crowded people, sense the spiritual atmosphere, and within seconds, pick out an individual who she has a clear prophetic word for. When she meets someone new, she 'susses' them out very quickly.

Strengths: You have the ability to push through obvious barriers.

You are often the one to take the lead.
You are commonly right about the way that something will turn out.
Once you encounter the truth of God, little will stop you.

Weaknesses:
You tend to overvalue your 'knowing' and leave others behind.
You may have a hard time valuing those who hear God differently.
You may miss it when God changes direction and does a new thing.

HEARERS tend to 'hear' God speak in words, possibly audibly, but most often inaudibly, as a still small voice. They listen to what the Holy Spirit is saying, often keeping journals to record the revelation they receive. Over time, 'hearers' develop a keen sense of recognizing God's voice.

This is the most common way that God speaks to me. As I described at the beginning of this chapter, I often sit with a notebook or journal and wait on God to give me a word. It generally begins with a simple thought or phrase and grows from there. I'll explain this process in greater detail in a later chapter.

Strengths: You work independently and keep to the word you heard.
You have a special way of hearing what others can't hear.
You can point to different times in your past when you have heard God clearly and this grounds your confidence in Him.

Weaknesses: Sometimes you don't see the details.
The message can get clouded by your own thoughts/filters.

Independence and lack of ability to work in a team.

FEELERS tend to experience the emotions of God. It's as if the Father expresses His heart through theirs. They feel things deeply and are very sensitive to the emotions of other people. When 'feelers' walk into a physical environment, they can often 'pick up' on what is going on. They find it difficult to explain, but 'feelers' just sense the spiritual atmosphere. God often interrupts them as they are going throughout their day. Often, but not always, 'feelers' also have the gift of intercession.

The story I told in the previous chapter was a perfect example of a 'feeler'. The prophet had hugged the man tightly, expressing the Father's love tangibly and breaking through years of pain and rejection.

Strengths: You feel what God feels.
You pick up on spiritual moments that others might miss.

Weaknesses: Can have difficulty functioning if everything doesn't "feel" right.
You overvalue subjective feelings.
You can be oversensitive to what others think/say.
You carry others' negative emotions at times.

SEERS tend to be very visual. God communicates with them through pictures, visions and dreams. They are often highly expressive individuals who are faith-filled. They dream big and see how things should be from Heaven's perspective. 'Seers' tend to be very certain when God has shown them something and will act on it without a lot of hesitation or deliberation.

Back in 2017, when we were first asked to lead HOPE Church, we politely declined. It was located in the town where I had grown up. When I had moved on from there 25 years ago, I did so without any intention of returning. Plus, we knew this church had been through a difficult journey and we really wanted somewhere without a chequered history.

However, God had other ideas.

Surprisingly, within a few weeks of declining the invitation from HOPE, something in our hearts began to shift. Perhaps we needed to be more open to the possibility. However, that wasn't enough to convince us to change our minds.

Around the same time, Becky kept telling me about numerous pictures and dreams she was having in which she would see a large white house with a treehouse in the garden.

Becky has a lot of pictures and dreams so, I have to confess, I didn't give these much attention. They didn't make sense to me. I didn't even know anyone who owned a white house as she had described.

Then, a week or two later, a couple with whom I went to high school, posted on Facebook that they were moving to New Zealand for one year and that their house would be available to rent. This house was 1 mile from HOPE Church.

Guess what color it was? White. And what was in the garden? A huge treehouse.

Immediately Becky was convinced that this was where God was calling us.

We met the leaders of the church and viewed our friend's house. Within two months we had moved into their house and had started leading the church. That was almost three years ago, and we have experienced so much favor and blessing in this place.

Strengths: You see beyond what most people see. You have long-distance vision.
You are often entrusted with big dreams.
You believe that anything is possible.
You have faith and longevity for your vision.

Weaknesses: You may grow weary or disillusioned when what you see doesn't happen as quickly as you expected.

You can have a hard time relating to those who don't see you what you see.

You can have a hard time valuing the ordinary, practical, day-to-day.

Do any of the above forms of hearing from God especially resonate with you?

Of course, you might hear God in a number of different ways. Most people are a combination of two or three of the above. But you will probably find that there is one dominant way that God most frequently speaks to you.

(Note: Havilah Cunnington from Bethel Church in Redding has a course called 'Prophetic Personalities' in which she explores this subject in greater detail.)

FILTERS: HOW YOU PROCESS WHAT GOD SAYS

So, these are the four primary forms or modes in which God will speak to you. However, we all have filters through which we individually interpret what we hear, feel, see, etc. A certain picture or word that means something significant to you could mean something completely different to someone else. You simply both process it differently, according to your personalities.

South African prophet, Julian Adams, describes the following five different personality filters through which we interpret what God says:

EXPRESSIVE: Expressive personalities take isolated incidents as signs in and of themselves. They view things as 'obviously God' that others might not immediately recognize.

For example, just a few days ago, my wife and I were driving to a hotel for an overnight break. The journey which should have taken 40 minutes took close to two hours. There were roadworks, a car accident, traffic jams and other diversions. I was feeling frustrated and annoyed. I just wanted to arrive at our destination.

As soon as we got to the hotel and checked in, we were informed that we had been upgraded to the best suite in the entire hotel, at no extra cost. We hadn't even asked for an upgrade. We had paid just over $300. The room they gave us cost around $1000 a night! Immediately I wanted to know what God was saying through this. The words I heard where: "It was worth the wait." God wanted to communicate that even though we go through delays and diversions in seeing prayers answered and promises fulfilled, when things do shift, it will be worth the wait.

As an expressive, this seemed obvious to me. My wife, on the other hand, was just excited by the huge, stand-alone bath! Expressives might notice things, as they go about their day to day lives, that others miss. For example, some of you keep seeing double numbers like two 11's or a word or phrase continually popping up. That's how God gets the attention of an 'expressive' personality.

CONTEMPLATIVE: Contemplative personalities look for patterns rather than isolated incidents. They take time to allow what they see, hear or sense to be processed as they seek increased clarity from the Lord. This often looks like journaling, praying or sharing the word/picture etc. with a trusted friend.
Contemplatives like to gather all of the information before they make a decision. They mull things over and over, first internally, and then perhaps with one or two others. Once they solidify their thinking around a revelation, they are rarely moved or dissuaded.

STRATEGIC: Strategic personalities view words/signs/ pictures etc in relation to how they contribute to the wider vision. They think pragmatically in terms of steps towards an end goal or destination. It's almost as if each sign is part of an overall puzzle and is only significant in relation to how it fits with all of the other pieces.

Strategic personalities place a lot of emphasis on wisdom, both human and divine. They want to position the right people in the right places the accomplish the vision. They have the ability to recognize moments of favor and opportunity and seize them.
I have a friend who owns a successful business and is also the trustee of a large church. While he is full of faith and loves to see God move in supernatural ways, being a strategic personality, he is constantly thinking about how all the pieces fit together to move everyone towards the vision. While still only in his 30's, he carries wisdom and responsibility far beyond his years.

ADVENTUROUS: Adventurers see signs as clues that they must follow, allowing the journey to unfold spontaneously as they go. They enjoy the twists and turns of the journey more than reaching the destination.
Adventurers are on a mission to discover. Like a spiritual Indiana Jones, they are always looking for maps, clues and signposts that will lead them towards the treasure that God has hidden for them.

MYSTICAL: Mystical personalities tend to be more focused on what is happening in the invisible/spiritual realm than on what is right in front of them. They love to have supernatural encounters and see almost everything as having some spiritual significance. Mystical personalities love 'wasting time' with Jesus. They sense subtle changes in the spiritual atmosphere quicker than other people. As well as being attuned to what God is doing, they are also very aware of the activity and actions of the enemy. They 'see' things in the spiritual world that are completely invisible to others.

As you discover your prophetic personality, remember that it is never set in stone. God loves to speak to His children in new ways in different seasons of our lives. Be open to changing, growing and developing throughout the course of your life.

Also, the way God communicates with you might even vary depending on what environment you are in. For example, the way God speaks to me when I am praying individually with people is different from how He tends to speak to me when I am ministering to a congregation from the front of a church. I *see* more when I am with individuals and *hear* more in a corporate setting.

The wonderful thing about the church is that God has placed together many different people who hear Him in very various ways. No one has the whole picture. We need each other if we are to discover the full revelation of the Lord.

Practical Exercise: Read through the various prophetic forms and filters again and underline the descriptions which immediately made you think: 'That's me.' Perhaps study them

with someone close to you and discuss how your different ways of hearing God might complement one another.

DAY 6

HOW GOD SPEAKS: THE BIBLE

"Anyone who wants to hear God's voice on a regular basis will have to become intimately acquainted with the written Word of God....Anyone who ignores the Bible is inviting deception and disaster to be his intimate companions in the journey of life."

(Jack Deere)

A few days ago, I shared how God directed us to the church we currently lead through my wife's visions and dreams of a white house with a treehouse. While this was certainly significant, there were many other prophetic confirmations that this was the right move for us.

Around the same time, one evening in our church small group, we were sharing prophetic words with one another. A young man in the gathering said: "Craig, the only thing God has given me for you is a verse from 1st Kings 19. It says, "Go back the way you came."

I smiled politely and thanked him. However, inwardly I groaned. At that point, I didn't want to go back the way I came! I was trying to avoid returning to my hometown. I tried to ignore his word. He could have been wrong after all.

A week or so later, Becky and I were having dinner and I decided to share with her what this guy had said. "Oh no," she responded. "I suppose I'm going to have to tell you now. A few weeks ago in a meeting, someone approached me and said they had a verse they felt that they needed to share. They weren't exactly where it was from in the Bible, but the verse was, "Go back the way you came."

Such a short and simple verse of Scripture, yet God used it to speak directly into our current situation. The *logos* had become a *rhema*.

LOGOS AND RHEMA WORDS

The Greek word *logos* simply means 'word'. As believers, *logos* refers principally to the entire written word of God, the Bible. It is absolutely authoritative and divinely inspired as 2 Tim 3: 16-17 reminds us:

"All Scripture is God-breathed and is useful for teaching, rebuking, correcting and training in righteousness, so that the servant of God may be thoroughly equipped for every good work."

Since the closing of the biblical canon (the 66 books of the Bible), God's partnership with us through prophecy is no longer a matter of establishing the *logos*. We have the fullness of the word of God to live from. It is settled forever in Heaven. It can never be added to or subtracted from by either human or angel.

In the Bible we discover God's character, ways, plan and eternal purpose. It is the absolute standard by which all other expressions, doctrines, beliefs, concepts, morals, decrees, and prophecies are measured.

Rhema, on the other hand, might be called "a word from the Lord" or "a spoken word". This happens when God's Spirit takes a *logos* and speaks directly and relevantly into a present situation bringing clarity, confirmation, insight and direction.

The word *rhema* is used 73 times in the New Testament. Here are some examples:

"Man shall not live on bread alone, but on every word (rhema) that comes from the mouth of God." (Matthew 4: 4)

"If you remain in me and my words (rhema) remain in you, ask whatever you wish, and it will be done for you." (John 15: 7)

"Take the helmet of salvation and the sword of the Spirit, which is the word (rhema) of God." (Ephesians 6: 17)

Have you ever been reading the Bible, when a particular verse seems to leap off the page as if highlighted? You may even have read it many times before, but on this occasion it takes on a whole new level of significance. This could very well be the *logos* becoming a *rhema* word especially for you.

Prophet Bill Hamon helpfully describes it like this: "The *Logos* is like a well of water, and the *rhema* is a bucket of water from that well. The *Logos* is like an entire piano, and the *rhema* is one note sounding forth from it. The *Logos* is like the whole human body, and the *rhema* is one of that body's members performing a particular function. The *rhema* is always dependent on the *Logos*…"

As Christians, we live by the *Logos*. It is the standard of all truth. But we also long for the *rhema,* a precise word for a specific situation.

THE POWER OF THE WORD OF GOD

I was preaching on a Sunday evening from Mark 5 about the healing of the daughter of Jairus. In the middle of the story, Jesus is interrupted by a woman with a debilitating bleeding condition. I had planned to skim over those verses as they weren't especially relevant to the key point I wanted to communicate. However, as I read the words in verse 29, "Immediately her bleeding stopped and she felt in her body that she was freed from her suffering", something stirred inside me.

Without really thinking about it, I looked up at the congregation of around 300 people and said: "There is a young lady in the room tonight who has a similar condition to the woman in this story. The Lord is going to heal you tonight."

Then I simply moved on with the rest of my message.

I had been reading the *logos*, but in that moment, the Holy Spirit gave me a *rhema*.

To be honest, I didn't give too much thought about what had happened. This type of medical condition is something most men want to steer away from.

Three months later, I was walking through town. Across the road, a lady from the church waved at me. She was with her daughter who, I'm guessing, was in her early 20's. I waved back and walked on, but then I heard the lady call my name. I stopped and waited, as they both crossed the road.

"Craig, I'm so glad we bumped into you," said the mother. "My daughter wants to tell you something. Normally she would be really embarrassed to share this, but she said she wants you to know."

I looked at the daughter, not sure what to expect.

"Do you remember when you were preaching back in October and you stopped your message and gave a word about a woman with a bleeding condition who God was going to heal?"

"Yes, I remember that," I nodded.

"Well, that was me. Obviously I'm not going to go into the details, but for a long, long time I had that problem. I had so many tests, but the consultants couldn't figure out what was wrong. I was actually getting really depressed, thinking I might have to live with this for the rest of my life. That Sunday night, however, when you gave that prophetic word, the bleeding stopped. Since then, everything has been completely normal."

Isn't that incredible?

In that moment, a *logos* became a *rhema* and a young woman was instantly healed.

God's Word is so incredibly powerful.

EAT THE WORD, SPEAK THE WORD

It is difficult to overemphasize the importance of feeding yourself daily on the Word of God. It is your spiritual nourishment, imparting supernatural life and fuel into your spirit. Sadly, too many Christians listen to a message in church on Sunday but rarely take time to really study the Scriptures during the week. Then they wonder why their lives are so devoid of the presence of God and why they struggle so much with sin. No matter how amazing your Sunday lunch is, you still need to eat healthy meals every day if you are to keep up your energy and strength.

Psalm 19: 7-8 tells us what God's Word does in our lives:

"The law of the LORD is perfect,
refreshing the soul.
The statutes of the LORD are trustworthy,
making wise the simple.
The precepts of the LORD are right,
giving joy to the heart.
The commands of the LORD are radiant,
giving light to the eyes."

We miss out on so much if we neglect the Word of God. It brings stability and success into our lives.

After the death of Moses, God instructed Joshua to lead the people into the Promised Land. I'm sure this was an incredibly daunting task. Yet, the Lord told Joshua that the secret to being successful was not going to be in his leadership skills or his experience. God commanded him:

"Be strong and very courageous. Be careful to obey all the law my servant Moses gave you; do not turn from it to the right or to the left, that you may be successful wherever you go. Keep this Book of the Law always on your lips; meditate on it day and night, so that you may be careful to do everything written in it. Then you will be prosperous and successful."

(Joshua 1: 7-8)

Within days of becoming a Christian in my mid-teens, someone gave me a Bible and a little booklet called 'Every Day with Jesus'. I was encouraged to have a daily 'quiet time' in which I would read the Bible and pray. This discipline soon became a delight that I rarely missed. Thirty years later I attribute so much of the Lord's blessing on my life as being a direct result of those early years of regularly feeding on His Word.

Scripture also provides us with 'guardrails' for the prophetic. In fact, chaos is often the result when we divorce the prophetic from the Scriptures. I'm sure most of you have heard horror stories of people who have said that God told them to do something that was so obviously contradictory to His Word, will and character.

There is no better way to learn how God speaks than by reading His Word. If you were to come to me and share something my wife had allegedly told you, immediately I would know if you were telling the truth. Over the years, I have grown to know her character and how she speaks. I would be able to say, "That sounds just like Becky," or, "Sorry, but I know she wouldn't say anything like that."

Similarly, if we are to learn to recognize the voice of God, there is no better way than by reading His Word on a consistent basis. It is the unchanging source of His voice. When we hear Him speak to us prophetically, we will immediately be able to discern if this sounds like something God would say. Does it line up with His character as revealed in Scripture?

Before bringing a 'now' word from God, we need to be building our lives on the 'eternal Word'. Then and only then can we safely, powerfully and consistently be trusted with the gift of the prophetic.

I know that we all have seasons when we struggle to read our Bibles. Our lives are so busy and full of distractions. We can end up feeling so guilty and condemned for our lack of discipline. Yet, if we were to really grasp the power that lies within the pages of this one Book, I believe we would make it a much greater priority in our lives.

Most things in life are temporary and fleeting. But the Word of God will stand forever and ever. It is our foundation stone, the truth against which we must set all our decisions. It is our standard for purity and integrity. It is a shield protecting us from the enemy's attacks and a sword that cuts through lies and torment. The Word of God is water that cleanses and refreshes and it is light that guides and directs us on the path of life. Like medicine, it can restore our souls, heal our bodies, and comfort those who are broken-hearted. God's Word is a seed that carries within it incredible potential for growth and an abundant harvest and it is bread that feeds and satisfies us.

There is a reason why the Bible is one of the few books throughout history to have been repeatedly banned or burned by governments and regimes because of its dangerous and subversive content. In fact, in just the past week in Portland, protesters burned a stack of Bibles in front of the federal courthouse. Clearly, some people see this book as a threat to their agenda.

Yet, rarely has there been a time when the world has been so desperate for solid, stable believers who are Spirit-filled and Scripture-soaked. When everything around us is being shaken, our cities, communities and neighbors are longing to hear a voice that offers stability, hope, healing, courage and truth.

Practical Exercise:

Read Psalm 23 (below) slowly two or three times.

Ask God to highlight one particular verse (or portion of a verse) specifically for you today.

Meditate on it, as you apply it to your own current situation.

Now, pray it over your life.

For example, it could simply be the line in verse 1: "I lack nothing."

Where do you feel any sense of lack or inadequacy in your life right now?

Thank God that He is your source and provider. Pray that verse specifically over the area where you feel deficient. Prophesy it over your life: "I lack nothing because God will abundantly provide for my every need."

Now repeat the above exercise, but this time, for someone you know.

As the Spirit leads you to a verse for them, why not send a message? You might well be amazed at how they respond!

Psalm 23

¹ The LORD is my shepherd, I lack nothing.
²   He makes me lie down in green pastures,
he leads me beside quiet waters,
³   he refreshes my soul.
He guides me along the right paths
    for his name's sake.
⁴ Even though I walk
    through the darkest valley,

I will fear no evil,
> for you are with me;
> your rod and your staff,
> they comfort me.
> ⁵ You prepare a table before me
> in the presence of my enemies.
> You anoint my head with oil;
> my cup overflows.
> ⁶ Surely your goodness and love will follow me
> all the days of my life,
> and I will dwell in the house of the LORD
> for ever.

DAY 7

HOW GOD SPEAKS: IMPRESSIONS

"Our bodies are designed to recognize and enjoy the presence of God. We can taste, see, smell, hear and touch in the Spirit! We must train our senses so that we do not miss our time of visitation."

(Julian Adams)

It was 12.55 pm. I had plans to meet a friend for lunch at 1.00 pm and was already running a few minutes behind. As I drove through a large housing development, I passed the home of a family who were nominal members of the church I was leading at that time. By 'nominal', I mean that they never attended church but were on our 'books'. As far as I knew, they weren't believers. I had only incidentally met them once around a year before.

Yet as I drove past the house, I had a subtle inner prompting that I should stop and call with them. I checked my watch. I really didn't have time, so I drove on. Yet, the feeling persisted. In my mind I protested, "But I hardly know them." I kept going. But the internal feeling wouldn't go away. Reluctantly, I turned the car around and texted my friend, explaining that I'd be a little late for lunch.

I walked up to the door and rang the bell. The lady who lived there answered and, upon seeing me standing there, immediately burst into tears. "Come in," she said. Her husband was sitting alone in the living room looking anxious and anguished. As I sat on their sofa, the lady explained that some routine medical results for her husband had come back that morning. A significant abnormality had shown up in a scan and her husband was being fast-tracked for an emergency biopsy later that afternoon. They were terrified. I spent a few moments with them, praying for complete health and wholeness throughout the man's body. As I was leaving, his wife said these words: "God must have sent you here today Craig. We didn't know where to turn or what to do. We just needed someone to pray with us. Thank you."

IT'S SO SUBTLE

I'm sure that you too have experienced those inner promptings at times. Those little nudges that you should call someone, send a text message, pray for a friend, give someone money. They are so subtle and easy to ignore. They're almost like a butterfly landing on your arm. It only rests there for a moment, you can barely feel it, and then it flies away. Yet, when you do respond, it's incredible how often you'll hear the other person say something like, "How did you know?" or "You've no idea just how much I needed that today."

In Mark 2:8 we read:

"Immediately *Jesus knew in his spirit* that this was what they were thinking in their hearts..."

That's what a prophetic impression is – a knowing in your spirit. It's the most simple form of revelation from God. There's no audible voice or inner vision. It's just a subtle sense in a moment that you need to take an action or that something is happening in your environment.

I believe that every Christian hears God speak to them through impressions. Often, however, they will feel more like simple intuition or random thoughts. And while they are similar, the difference is the source. A prophetic impression comes to us through the Holy Spirit. In fact, sometimes a prophetic impression will tell us the opposite from what we are observing with our eyes or hearing with our ears. Someone, for instance, might look like they are in perfect health, yet inexplicably, you have a sense you should pray about a medical condition.

GOD SPEAKS THROUGH YOUR SENSES

As humans, we have five senses: sight, hearing, touch, smell and taste. Often, in the prophetic, we focus on seeing and hearing. God, however, created us to communicate with Him through all of our senses. Just as we can subtly detect an unusual smell or sound, so too we can sense small spiritual shifts in the atmosphere or communications from Heaven.

While these impressions may be less precise than a prophetic word or vision, they are no less effective. Often, in church, I'll simply get a sense that we should pray for a particular medical condition. I may just feel a pain in my knee or heat on my hands that weren't there before. This is one of the main ways we have seen people healed in our services.

I have a good friend who, when he is around someone who is struggling with pornography, will begin to feel a burning sensation in his thighs. At first, he thought this was totally bizarre and had no idea what was happening. However, over time, as he has learned to discern what God is saying, he has been able to bring freedom and deliverance to many people. The key is to pay attention to these slight changes in your body.

God will also speak through impressions in your emotions. You may be around someone and unexpectedly begin to feel what they are feeling. For example, in a restaurant, when the server comes to your table, you may inexplicably begin to feel grief or sorrow. God might be allowing you to feel what they are feeling so that you can minister His love and healing to them.

It can also happen when praying for someone. You may find yourself overwhelmed with some sort of emotion for them. God is expressing His feelings for them through you.

Once, when I was praying for a young man in a church where I had been the guest preacher, I began to get a really 'icky' feeling, almost like I was dirty or disgusted with myself. I prayed into any shame or guilt this individual might be feeling because of something they had done. The young man broke down and later indicated he had engaged in a homosexual act in the recent past which he now deeply regretted. As he wept in repentance, I was able to break off all demonic influence and reaffirm his identity as a man of God.

God can even speak to you through your sense of smell. It could be a pungent odor indicating a demonic presence or a pleasant fragrance as God's presence is highlighted to you. Occasionally, as I have been ministering to someone, I have smelled something that reminded me of something or someone else. For example, it could be a perfume or the smell of an old building or the ocean. Again, in those moments, you need to ask the Holy Spirit what He is showing you.

Impressions like these can come at any time. You don't need to be in church or even praying. You simply need to be open and attentive to the Holy Spirit as you go about your day.

Nehemiah told how God led him through an impression as they completed the rebuilding of the walls of Jerusalem: "*So my God put it into my heart* to assemble the nobles, the officials and the common people for registration by families." (Nehemiah 7:5) He simply had an inner impression in his heart that came from God.

When Paul was preaching in Lystra, there was a man there who had been lame since birth. As he was looking at the man, he "saw that he had faith to be healed." (Acts 14: 9) How do you *see* faith? Paul obviously had some sort of spiritual perception or impression about the man.

One reason why many Christians don't hear God speak more often is that they treat these prophetic impressions as just their 'feelings' and so they ignore them. This is especially true of people who are more logical, rational and analytical. We have been taught that feelings are fickle and unreliable. We need to focus on thoughts and facts, not feelings. Yet, God created us with feelings, and He will often bypass our minds to reveal His heart.

THE BIG IS IN THE SMALL

The Bible makes it clear that God will test us with a little before He entrusts us with much (Luke 16: 10). Impressions or divine nudges may seem like a less exciting or lower-level form of prophesy than visions and dreams, but they are used by God to increase our spiritual sensitivity and to demonstrate our obedience.

Impressions may not always be about ministering to someone else. God could use them to speak to you about your own situation. For example, at times, your feelings might become heightened. One moment you're completely fine, the next you feel a deep sense of foreboding or anxiety. It's almost as if a warning light has been switched on. You have no idea where it came from, but you do know that you need to pray. When that happens to me, I will often pray for angels to surround me, break any assignment of the enemy against me, and plead the blood of Jesus over me and my family. I will also pray in tongues until the foreboding lifts. On at least two occasions that I am aware of, I have narrowly missed major road traffic accidents after responding in prayer like this.

I should also state at this point that **not every feeling is from the Holy Spirit.** Some people are, by nature, much more emotional than others. Others are deeply wounded or self-centred. If they followed every feeling that they had throughout the day, they would end up in all sorts of trouble!

Impressions can be very real and from the Lord, but they are also on a level that can easily be influenced by our own feelings, assumptions, or presumptions. Therefore, I think anything received on this level should be prefaced with "I think," "I feel" or "I'm sensing," rather than "thus saith the Lord." Don't be surprised or discouraged if you feel something strongly and it turns out to be wrong. Just resolve that you are going to learn from the experience.

Over time, through discipline and wisdom, as we learn to discern the voice of God in our feelings, minds and bodies, we can become more effective ministers of God's grace and mercy.

GOD RELEASED PROVISION THROUGH IMPRESSIONS

A few years ago, after we left our safe, secure jobs in Dublin and moved to the north coast of Ireland for a year, money was very tight for our family. One particular month we had some unexpected bills and simply didn't have enough to pay for rent, food and petrol. I didn't know what to do except pray and trust God. It sounds so simple, but I was becoming really stressed at the thought that I wasn't going to be able to provide for my family.

Completely out of the blue, on a Friday evening, a text message came through from an old friend who I hadn't spoken to for around five years. It simply said, "Hi Craig, can you send me your bank details?" I replied, joking, "If you're trying to steal from me, good luck!" I did as he asked and within ten minutes he had deposited £500 into my account. I was stunned. Apparently, he had been sitting watching TV with his wife and had felt prompted that he should give us some money.

Two days later, on Sunday morning, I was walking out of church. A man who I barely knew stopped me at the door and handed me an envelope. He said, "Will you give this to your wife? I was going to give this to you, but the Lord told me I was to give it to Becky." When she opened it, inside was another £500.

In the space of a few days, through two people simply responding to those subtle divine nudges, God had more than provided for our immediate needs. As well as being overwhelmed with gratitude, God also taught me just how important it is to be obedient in those moments. It may not seem like much at the time, but it can change someone's life.

Practical Exercise: Today, as you go about your normal routine, ask God to increase your spiritual sensitivity to those little divine 'nudges' and impressions. Have the courage to act on them. Send that text message. Pray for that person. Speak that word of encouragement. Hand someone the cash in your purse.

You could be wrong. That's okay. But you might also express God's heart to someone who really needs to know His love today. Take the risk.

DAY 8

HOW GOD SPEAKS: THE VOICES OF GOD

"The Lord is more determined and excited to speak to us than we are to hear from Him."

(Kris Vallotton)

George Jeffreys was a famous Welsh minister who founded the Elim Pentecostal Church. He dedicated his life to Christ during the Welsh revival of 1904. Six years later he was baptized in the Holy Spirit. A new power came upon him and he began to preach all over the place with many coming to faith in Jesus. He was one of the most anointed preachers and evangelists the UK ever had.

Fast forward to 1962.

All of you will have heard of Billy Graham, but not everyone has heard of Reinhard Bonnke. And yet he was the greatest evangelist of our generation before he went to be with Jesus in December 2019. He saw more people receive salvation through his evangelistic crusades than any other person in the last 100 years.

When Reinhard was 22 years old, he had just graduated from Bible College in London and had a free day to do whatever he chose. He decided to spend it in the city and take in the sights. He got on board one of the famous red double-decker buses, and as the vehicle was moving along, all of a sudden at Clapham, he felt the Holy Spirit say to him: "Get off this bus".

He obeyed the prompting and found himself just walking along one of the streets of London, not quite sure where he was. Then he came upon a plaque on the gate of a house and it read "George Jeffreys".

He wondered to himself if this could be the house of the great George Jeffreys, the man who shook England in the 1920's and 30's. He knew from his studies that George Jeffreys was considered England's greatest evangelist, after John Wesley and George Whitefield.

Reinhard was unsure and it was then that the Holy Spirit said to him: "You will never know if you don't ask." So he knocked on the door and a woman answered it. Bonnke asked if the house belonged to George Jeffreys, the famous evangelist who preached throughout England in the 1940's. She said yes.

"Is he alive?"
"Yes."

"Does he live in this house?"
"Yes."
"Is he now in the house?"
"Yes."
"Can I see him?"
"No."

And it was then that he heard a deep voice coming from the inside: "Let him come in".

When Reinhard walked in, he saw a frail old man sitting there. After some introductions and a brief chat, Mr. Jeffreys laid his hands upon Bonnke and blessed him. He staggered out of the house because the presence of God was so tangibly resting upon him.

Bonnke then left to return to Germany the next day. His father met him at the railway station and after exchanging some pleasantries, his father said: "Reinhard, did you hear the news? George Jeffreys just passed away."

"No, that can't be," Reinhard replied, "I was just with the man."

And then, all of a sudden, he realized that he caught something from the previous generation. One generation was passing and handing over their mantle to the next generation.

When I read a story like that, I can't help but wonder: what if Reinhard hadn't heard God's voice that day? Or what if he had chosen to ignore it?

When God speaks, it not only impacts our own lives, but it can literally change the destiny of countless others through how God uses us.

THE THREE VOICES OF GOD

How did Reinhard Bonnke 'hear' God speak on that eventful day? Did a booming voice thunder from Heaven? I don't think so. It's more likely that he heard the quiet, inner voice of the Lord.

When the talk about hearing 'the voice of the Lord', we need to know that He speaks in three different voices:

(i)   The Still, Small Voice

This is the internal, inaudible voice of God. It's definitely how I hear God most regularly. It can be like a soft and gentle whisper that comes as we spend time in prayer and silence. Most often, for me, it simply comes in the form of a thought, a word or a phrase in my mind. In fact, the most helpful piece of advice I ever received about hearing God's voice was this: **'God's voice usually sounds very much like your thoughts.'**

(Let me immediately add a disclaimer here: not every thought you have is God speaking to you!)

Many of my posts on Daily Prophetic start in this way. Often when God speaks to me, it comes in the form of a thought that I wouldn't naturally have. It can seem a bit random. For example, I might wake up with a line from a song going through my mind, even though I haven't listened to that song in years. Or I may hear a phrase like: "It's time to get up and walk" or "It's coming around again."

I will then write that word or phrase in my journal and ask God to show me more. Sometimes that involves sitting in silence and listening. Alternatively, I might pray in tongues quietly. Generally, as I do this, more related words and sentences will form in my mind related to the initial phrase. At this point, I don't filter any of it. I just want to get it all down on paper. Frequently a verse or passage of Scripture will also come to mind as I continue to listen and reflect.

After I've written everything that I believe the Lord has given me, I might leave it for a while and come back to it later. Occasionally a few more related thoughts will come into my mind. Then, at some point, I form the related phrases and sentences into a longer prophetic word. This might be typed but often I use a dictation app on the my phone and simply begin to speak it out.

The still, small voice of God generally comes to bring personal instruction or encouragement. In 1 Kings 19, the prophet Elijah is in a very low place. He is physically, emotionally and spiritually exhausted. He's used to hearing God speak in dramatic ways. However, this time we read:

"Then a great and powerful wind tore the mountains apart and shattered the rocks before the LORD, but the LORD was not in the wind. After the wind there was an earthquake, but the LORD was not in the earthquake. After the earthquake came a fire, but the LORD was not in the fire. And after the fire came a gentle whisper. When Elijah heard it, he pulled his cloak over his face and went out and stood at the mouth of the cave.

Then a voice said to him, 'What are you doing here, Elijah?'" (vv. 11-13)

You will notice that the text distinguishes between the 'gentle whisper' that Elijah heard inside the cave and the voice of God that he heard when he walked outside. One was clearer and more obvious than the other.

While this is a totally valid way that God speaks, it must be remembered that it is highly subjective and can be heavily influenced by the desires of our own hearts i.e. God only says what we want to hear. As always, it must line up with what we know about God's will and character as revealed in in the Bible and it should also be grounded in some sort of current reality. Don't make life-changing decisions based on one experience of hearing God's still, small voice.

(ii) The Internal, Audible Voice of God

This is more clear and obvious than the still, small voice. It doesn't so much come in our thoughts as it cuts right through them. It's almost as if God shouts something from inside us and we have to stop and pay attention. Although it's not audible, it's so unmistakeable that it feels as if it was shouted out loud.

I believe that the internal, audible voice of God is what we see described when the Bible says:

"The word of the LORD came to…" (e.g. 1 Samuel 15: 10; 1 Kings 13: 20; Ezekiel 14: 2)

God is speaking clearly to the prophet, but it is distinguished from His audible voice that we read about in passages such as Exodus 6: 13:

"…the LORD spoke to Moses and Aaron…"

The internal, audible voice of God is different than simply hearing Him communicate through our own thoughts. There is a greater clarity, weight and authority when God speaks to us in this manner.

I was once asked to speak at a large church that was going through significant transition. A few weeks beforehand, I was suddenly awakened at around 4.00 am. Immediately God began to speak so clearly the message I was to bring to this congregation, and especially the leadership. I literally jumped out of bed, ran to my study, and began to write down what He was saying. For the next 30 minutes, it was as if God dictated or downloaded the entire message word for word. While it wasn't audible to anyone else, it seemed as if God was beside me in the room talking directly to me. I didn't have to study or prepare. I just shared what God said. Five years later, the leaders of that church tell me that they often refer back to my message from that weekend because it spoke so powerfully and clearly into their situation.

(iii) The Audible Voice of God

This is obviously a clearer and higher level of revelation than hearing God speak internally. Often, it's not that the voice is actually audible, but to you, in that moment, it seems surprising that others can't hear it too. Steve Thompson, in his excellent book *You May All Prophesy*, puts it like this:

"When He speaks in this fashion, all thought and doubt are removed. It is not so much that it is loud in volume, but that it is immense in nature."

In Luke 9: 35, we read:

"A voice came from the cloud, saying, 'This is my Son, whom I have chosen; listen to him.'"

After God speaks like this, you don't *think* you heard God speak, you *know* for certain. There is no mistaking it. You are profoundly moved. It becomes a turning point in your life that you never forget.

Francis Schaeffer is one of the most credible Christian writers and leaders of the twentieth century. Early in his ministry, he faced a minor crisis. Francis and his young family needed temporary housing during a transition time but had very little money. They needed a "minor miracle" from the Lord. While Francis was praying about this, he said to God, "Where can we live, Lord? Please show us." Immediately, in response to his question, he heard an audible voice. It wasn't a voice inside of his mind. It didn't come from another human. He was alone. The voice simply said, "Uncle Harrison's house."

Although the answer was perfectly clear - it was an audible voice - it made no sense. Uncle Harrison had never given the Schaeffer family anything, and they thought it would be very unlikely he would offer his house for them to live in. Yet the voice that spoke to Francis was so startling and direct he felt he had to obey it. He wrote his uncle, asking him what he planned to do with his house for the next year. He was astonished when his uncle replied that he planned to live with his brother for the next year and would like to offer his house free of rent to Francis and his family for a year. Francis Schaeffer claims that this was the second time God had spoken to him in an audible voice.

I have personally never heard the audible voice of God. At least, not yet. And while I would love to, I'm also mindful of the words of Jack Deere:

"The clearer the revelation, the harder the task....When God speaks to you most clearly, it usually means you are going to go through such a difficult experience that later you will need to be absolutely certain that God had spoken to you. In fact, the clarity of the voice may be the main thing that gives you the power to endure the subsequent testing."

I wholeheartedly believe that God still speaks audibly today, however it is not the norm. While I know a few individuals who have heard Him speak in this manner, they rarely talk about it publicly. It marked a significant calling or transition in their lives that took great boldness and courage. At the time, they needed the absolute certainty of knowing that God had spoken to enable them to take the risks and face the challenges which lay ahead.

WE ARE POSITIONED TO HEAR HIS VOICE

It's helpful to remember that in the Old Testament, God was external to the people. To really meet with Yahweh, meant going to the holiest place in the temple. Access was granted to very few. Therefore, if and when God spoke, it was often externally and addressed to a particular individual assigned to a specific task.

However, as New Testament believers, cleansed by the blood of Christ, God now lives inside each one of us by His Spirit. Therefore, it is more likely that God will speak from within us. I believe that this is what Jesus meant when he said:

"I have much more to say to you, more than you can now bear. But when he, the Spirit of truth, comes, he will guide you into all the truth. He will not speak on his own; he will speak only what he hears, and he will tell you what is yet to come....the Spirit will receive from me what he will make known to you."

(John 16: 12-13; 15)

Paul also reminds us that "we have the mind of Christ." (1 Corinthians 2: 16)

As Kris Vollotton says:

"When we study the prophets of the Old Testament, we can easily become envious of how clearly they heard God's voice. However, Jesus makes it plain that those who are born again have a tremendous advantage over anyone who lived under the old covenant because God's Spirit now resides within us and is in constant communication with our spirit."

The indwelling Holy Spirit communicates with our human spirit and mind the thoughts and will of the Lord. As with any prophetic experience, the voice of God never comes to control or dominate us, but to invite us into greater freedom and fulness in the Father's love.

How is God speaking to you today?

Practical Exercise:

Find somewhere quiet where you won't be disturbed for 10 minutes. Bring a pen and a journal or blank sheet of paper.

Simply say: "God, what do you want to say to me today?"

Be still. Listen.

This is not about clearing your mind. It's inviting God to fill your mind.

Write down every thought that comes into your mind. Don't filter them or try to make sense of them. Just write.

If nothing comes, don't get stressed or tense. Just wait. As you wait in His presence expectantly, the Lord will speak.

Feel free to ask Him a specific question.

At the end of 10 minutes, read through what you've written and see if there are any common strands or a particular emphasis.

Practice this as often as possible and you will begin to find it easier to discern the voice of God.

DAY 9

HOW GOD SPEAKS: PICTURES AND VISIONS // PART 1

"The name for a prophet, in the olden time, was a "seer"- a man who could see, one who could see with his mind's eye, one who could also see with spiritual insight, so as vividly to realize the truth which he had to deliver in the name of the Lord. Learn that simple lesson well, O you who try to speak for God! You must be seers before you can be speakers."
(C. H. Spurgeon)

In my previous book, *The Tension of Transition*, I shared how a vivid prophetic vision in 2016 altered the course of our lives.

After five years of leading a church in inner-city Dublin, we had sensed for some time that God was moving us on. For months, I had been praying that a new door of opportunity would open for us. But nothing new was emerging.

In an early morning vision, I saw myself being released from a prison cell. As I nervously walked towards freedom, I had only one question on my mind: *Would there be anyone waiting for me on the outside?*

I had to keep moving.

Slowly, the huge steel prison gate slid open, and outside was a big car of smiling faces. They were waving at me, beckoning me forward.

The relief was overwhelming. There was someone waiting for me on the other side.

We will discuss this in more detail in a later chapter, but all prophecy has three aspects or components: **Revelation, Interpretation and Application.**

- **Revelation**: *What is God saying? What do you see, sense, hear?*

- **Interpretation**: *What does it mean? It's almost like translating God's language to yours.*

- **Application**: *What am I supposed to do with it? What does this practically mean?*

In this case, the revelation was the vision itself.

But what did it mean?

My prayer had been: *"God, will you open a door for us."*

In the vision, a prison door opened, so that makes some sense. God was opening a door.

However, it wasn't an *entrance* taking me into somewhere new. It was an *exit*, releasing me from somewhere I had been confined.

God seemed to be saying: "I am opening a door, but it's not what you think. I'm not telling you where you're going to be next, but I am releasing you from your current assignment of leading this church."

But that left the big question: *where were we to go?*

As I thought about the rest of the vision, I sensed God was saying clearly: "I am releasing you but I'm not telling you where you're going next. You will have to trust me. I will have someone waiting for you on the other side. You just need to keep walking. It's time to leave."

Within one week, through much prayer, various circumstances and many long conversations, the vision was clearly confirmed. We had to move on. We both resigned from our jobs and began a four-month sabbatical, with absolutely no idea what God had on the other side of this transition. But, as God had made clear in the vision, we simply had to keep walking.

If you've read *The Tension of Transition,* you will know how God incredibly opened a door for us at the end of our sabbatical. We spent a year on staff at an incredible church, Causeway Coast Vineyard, before I was asked to become Lead Pastor of HOPE Church, where we currently serve.

That vision happened four years ago, yet I still look back to it as being the most pivotal event in giving us the faith and courage to step into every new thing God has opened up for us, including starting Daily Prophetic and beginning to write books.

I would love to tell you that God leads me with clear, supernatural visions like this all the time, but that is simply not the case. I've been a Christian for 30 years and have only experienced a few of these in my life. As I said in an earlier chapter, I more of a *hearer* than a *seer*. However, I do believe God communicates with every believer through their visual senses.

YOU HAVE SPIRITUAL SIGHT

The Bible contains over 110 references to visions. Many of the Old Testament prophets received revelations in the form of imagery and moving pictures. However, visions aren't reserved for a select few special spokesmen. In fact, on the day of Pentecost, Peter declared that the words from the prophet Joel were now being fulfilled with the coming of the Holy Spirit:

"In the last days, God says,
I will pour out my Spirit on all people.
Your sons and daughters will prophesy,
your young men will see visions,
your old men will dream dreams."   (Acts 2: 17)

Supernatural visions should be normal for Spirit-filled believers. Along with other spiritual abilities, they come as part of the package when we receive salvation. Your spiritual eyes are opened. You can see in the Spirit. With that in mind, let's begin to explore different types of prophetic visions and pictures.

PROPHETIC GLIMPSES

These are fleeting internal pictures from the Lord. Literally, it's as if God gives us a snapshot of a person, place, or scene. Like prophetic words and impressions, these will be images or pictures that you would not have naturally thought of at that moment. While you will see them in your natural mind, they are from the Holy Spirit.

In Jeremiah 1 we read:

"The word of the LORD came to me: 'What do you see, Jeremiah?'

'I see the branch of an almond tree,' I replied.

The LORD said to me, 'You have seen correctly, for I am watching to see that my word is fulfilled.'

The word of the LORD came to me again: 'What do you see?'

'I see a pot that is boiling,' I answered. 'It is tilting towards us from the north.'

The LORD said to me, 'From the north disaster will be poured out on all who live in the land."

(vv. 11-14)

Before Jeremiah would speak for God, he was being taught to see. An almond tree and a boiling pot weren't the most elaborate, detailed visions. These were very simple pictures but God was using them to show Jeremiah something about the future for His people.

Sometimes when God gives you a picture, you will immediately recognize it as something familiar. Other times, it will make no sense at all. For example, when my wife had a picture of a white house with a treehouse, it meant nothing to either of us at the time. However, as soon as we saw the photographs of our friends' house, it all became very clear.

These pictures or images can be of almost anything. The face of a friend might pop into your mind for no reason. Could God be prompting you to reach out to them?

Oftentimes they will be symbolic in nature. You might see a red flashing light. Is God warning you about a situation ahead? Or

God might show you a picture of a packed suitcase. Is there a move happening soon?

When we first moved to Dublin, many people shared that in our Sunday services they had pictures of little green shoots coming up through hard soil. We interpreted that as God was bringing new life into a place that had become somewhat barren.

Often God will give you a picture when you are praying for others which may mean little to you at the time. It takes courage and faith to step out and share them.

I was once praying with a man at a conference and kept seeing an image of a horse. I shared it with him, expecting him to tell me he owned horses. Instead, he laughed out loud and told me his last name was 'Bridle'! Another time, as I prayed, I kept seeing a crown on a lady's head. God was wanting to remind her of her true identity - that she was a daughter of the King.

Sometimes God will visually show you a written word rather than a picture.

There is a well-known story that was told by John Wimber, founder of the Vineyard movement of churches. He was flying from Chicago to New York. It had been a long day and he was looking forward to some rest on the flight. Wimber describes what happened next:

"Seated across the aisle from me was a middle-aged man, a businessman, to judge from his appearance, but there was nothing unusual or noteworthy about him. But in the split second that my eyes happened to be cast in his direction, I saw something that startled me.

Written across his face in very clear and distinct letters I thought I saw the word "adultery." I blinked, rubbed my eyes, and looked again. It was still there. "Adultery." I was seeing it not with my eyes, but in my mind's eye. No one else on the plane, I am sure, saw it. It was the Spirit of God communicating to me. The fact that it was a spiritual phenomenon made it no less real."

God also revealed a woman's name to John Wimber. To condense the story, the two men talked privately in a separate part of the plane. The businessman admitted he had been having an affair with a woman of that name. He repented of his sin and told his wife what had happened. After much emotion and further conversation, they both accepted Christ into their lives.

Obviously, a prophetic revelation like this needs to be treated very carefully. Later in this book, we'll discuss prophetic wisdom and how we should share difficult words. However, the point is, a short picture of one single word 'adultery' unlocked the man's heart and led to salvation.

Another form of short visions is 'flashbacks'. Shawn Bolz describes them like this:

"A flashback is the instantaneous knowledge of God's past involvement in a person's life, place or thing."

A few years ago, our church organized an *Alpha Course*, designed to introduce non-believers to the Gospel. On the fifth week of the course, I asked if anybody would like prayer. As a few of us prayed with one young lady, I had a fleeting image of her walking in a field as a young girl, perhaps eight years old. She reached up and took her father's hand. That was all I saw.

I shared this picture with her. She immediately began to weep. Apparently, this young woman had grown up in rural Ireland where she had a difficult and lonely childhood. One day, when she was around eight years old, as she walked alone through a nearby field, feeling troubled and afraid, she had prayed for the very first time in her life. Immediately she became very aware of God's presence. So aware, she said, that she reached her little hand up in the air and asked God to hold it. Now, 20 years later, this simple 'flashback' unlocked her heart and she reconnected with her Heavenly Father.

If God speaks to you in 'flashbacks', you may find that you have many 'déjà vu' moments. You'll walk into a room and feel as if you've been there before. Or maybe you'll meet someone and think that you already know them or have had a particular conversation with them. It's possible that at some stage previously, you have received a prophetic snapshot of that person or the event in your mind.

INTERPRETATION IS KEY

Often receiving the picture or short vision is the easy part. The interpretation or 'what it means' can be more difficult to discern. For example, if you were praying for someone and saw a prophetic picture of a lion, what would immediately come to mind?

Jesus is called 'the lion of the tribe of Judah' in Revelation 5:5.

However, 1 Peter 5: 8 warns us, "Your enemy the devil prowls around like a roaring lion looking for someone to devour."

Which is it? An encouragement or a warning? That is where you will need to depend on the Holy Spirit to reveal what he is communicating in this specific situation.

There are also a number of 'prophetic dictionaries' that can be very useful in understanding what different symbols mean. My wife finds *The Divinity Code* by Adam Thompson helpful. Dr. Joe Ibojie has also written a number of books that come highly recommended.

As with every aspect of the prophetic, the most important thing is to actually step out and share what God is showing you. It may seem strange or ridiculous to you, but it could be powerful and profound to someone else. If you want to grow, there will be risk involved. You will get it wrong at times. However, the joy in seeing someone's face light up when they discover that God knows the intimate and intricate details of their life makes it all very worthwhile.

Practical Exercise: The next time you are praying with or for someone, be silent for a few moments and ask God for a picture. If anything pops into your mind which isn't a 'normal' thought, share it with them.

Just say something like: "When I was praying for you, I saw you surrounded by young people. Is working with kids something you do or would like to do?"

What's the worst that could happen?

If they say "no", you can simply say, "OK, thanks. I'm trying to learn to hear God speak better, so I'm taking risks when I think He is showing me something. He loves you so much. Thanks for letting me pray."

DAY 10

HOW GOD SPEAKS: PICTURES AND VISIONS // PART 2

"What makes us uniquely the people of God is that we are called to be people of the Spirit. Immersed in that Spirit, our speech changes, because our eyes, ears, and hearts have been opened to see beyond the world in front of our eyes to the world that lies behind what our eyes can see."
(Mark J. Chironna)

Not long ago, one Sunday evening following a church service where I had been the guest preacher, Becky and I were praying for a young lady in her mid-20's. As I stood quietly with my hand on her shoulder, I asked the Lord if there was anything He wanted to share with her.

Within moments, I had a vision of a girl in her late teens stumbling out of a nightclub. She was clearly intoxicated. I saw this in my mind, but it was as if I was right there, watching it happen.

All around, I could see bars and clubs, flashing signs, and crowds of young people. The scene immediately reminded me of a popular tourist resort in Spain that I had visited many years before. The girl in the vision was alone and visibly distraught. She looked around and not knowing what to do or where to go, she took her shoes off and sat on the edge of the pavement, her head in her hands, sobbing profusely.

I shared what I was seeing with the young lady. I also told her I believed that she was called to reach out to 'party girls' like the one I was seeing.

Somewhat stunned, she told me that this was exactly how she had become a Christian. In her late teens, she had been running from God, living a lifestyle of partying and drinking. One particular night, while on vacation in Spain, she had somehow become separated from her friends in a nightclub. Alone and afraid, she stumbled out of the club, fell to the ground, and cried out to God for help. That night became a turning point in her life.

There was more. She had already made plans to return to that exact tourist resort a few months later as part of a Christian mission team, to reach out to young people with the good news of Jesus. This was the confirmation she needed that she was making the right decision.

In the previous chapter, we began to explore how God speaks to us through pictures and visions. We focused on 'low-level' visions, where we receive a simple snapshot or brief picture of a person, place, or event. These are a very common way God communicates with His children.

Moving beyond these glimpses in the Spirit, the next step or stage of revelation would be:

INTERNAL VISIONS

This is what I have just described above. An internal vision is much stronger than a simple glimpse or snapshot. While it is still seen internally, there is more detail - movement, a scene, a storyline, a script of transpiring events. Some may be stronger and more vivid than others, therefore it is important to stay focused and undistracted so that you don't miss the details.

In Acts 9, immediately after his conversion, Paul had an internal vision:

"In a vision he has seen a man named Ananias come and place his hands on him to restore his sight."

This was more than just a quick snapshot. Paul saw a man, knew his name, and was also shown what he would do.

Often, when you receive an internal vision, you may well dismiss it, thinking that it's just your imagination. In reality, God is revealing something to what the Bible calls "the eyes of your heart." (Ephesians 1: 18) The word "heart" is sometimes translated as "understanding" or "mind". As a believer, you have double vision. You can see the visible world with your natural eyes, but also you can comprehend the spiritual world with the eyes of your heart.

Just this week, I was having coffee with a pastor friend. As we chatted about church and family, I kept seeing a map of mainland Europe in my mind. There were many dotted lines spanning out into the continent from Northern Ireland where we live. They looked like flight paths. I saw my friend in meetings, speaking to leaders, and sharing on platforms. I was fully present in the moment with him, yet at the same time, there was another series of moving images and thoughts in my mind. At the end of our meeting, I asked if he had ever considered leading a network of leaders in Europe. He said no, but that he had recently received a number of other prophetic words relating to Europe and a leadership role. Perhaps God was pointing to something new.

If I'm praying with someone and I receive an internal vision, I simply describe to them what I'm seeing in real-time. It may sound something like this: "I see you in a gym trying to lift a weight which is much too heavy. You're sweating and straining but it's not budging. Then someone walks over. You don't seem to know them. They tell you to adjust your grip slightly and when you do this, you can lift the weight without difficulty." Then I might ask the Lord what this means. As I receive the interpretation, I'll share it with them: "I believe there is an area of your life where you are feeling stuck or overwhelmed right now. You're trying your best, but nothing is changing. You're exhausted and ready to quit. But hold on. God is going to bring someone into your life who has wisdom to help you in this area. Listen to them. Small changes are going to significant results. Does this make any sense to you?"

Do you see what I did there? It wasn't mystical, weird, or complicated. I simply shared what I was seeing and interpreted it in a natural way. It was either going to be right or wrong. But overall, it was strengthening, encouraging and comforting to the recipient.

Could you do that too? Of course you could!

OPEN VISIONS

These visions are generally received when your eyes are open and are not easily stopped by distractions. You could be doing something else completely, such as driving, but in those moments the vision becomes more real to you than the world around you. The experience is similar to watching a scene acted out physically on a movie screen. It's not only in your mind or imagination, it's as if it is taking place right in front of you. It's that real.

The vision I shared in the previous chapter in which I was being released from a prison cell would fall into this category. Even though I was praying at the time, in those moments I was completely unaware of my surroundings. For maybe ten minutes, I literally felt as if I was fully experiencing what I was seeing.

Typically, when you have an open vision, you *know* that this was God speaking and it's not just your imagination. You don't 'snap out of it' until God has shown you everything that He wants you to see.

Sometimes you will also hear God's voice in the vision. A good example is Acts 10:

"About noon the following day as they were on their journey and approaching the city, Peter went up on the roof to pray. He became hungry and wanted something to eat, and while the meal was being prepared, he fell into a trance. He saw heaven opened and something like a large sheet being let down to earth by its four corners. It contained all kinds of four-footed animals, as well as reptiles and birds. Then a voice told him, 'Get up, Peter. Kill and eat.'

'Surely not, Lord!' Peter replied. 'I have never eaten anything impure or unclean.'

The voice spoke to him a second time, 'Do not call anything impure that God has made clean.'

This happened three times, and immediately the sheet was taken back to heaven." (vv. 9-16)

Notice it says, "Peter fell into a trance." While some people distinguish trances from open visions, I believe that they are incredibly similar. In both cases, you become unaware of your surroundings and are spiritually 'transported' into another realm for a few moments (or sometimes longer).

The entire book of Revelation is an open vision or trance that John had while exiled on the island of Patmos. The curtain was pulled back and the apostle was given open access to gaze into the invisible spiritual realm to see and hear what was happening, and also what was to come. From the length of the revelation that we have in our Bibles, and the huge amount of detail involved, John's vision probably lasted a few hours.

Sometimes an open vision can appear as something superimposed over the natural world. You can still see what is physical/visible, but you also equally see what is, to other people, spiritual/invisible. They are both as real as each other in that moment. For example, my wife will occasionally see angels in our church building or standing behind me as I preach. This is similar to what we read about in 2 Kings 6:

"When the servant of the man of God got up and went out early the next morning, an army with horses and chariots had surrounded the city. 'Oh no, my lord! What shall we do?' the servant asked.

'Don't be afraid,' the prophet answered. 'Those who are with us are more than those who are with them.'

And Elisha prayed, 'Open his eyes, LORD, so that he may see.' Then the LORD opened the servant's eyes, and he looked and saw the hills full of horses and chariots of fire all round Elisha." (vv. 15-17)

The horses and chariots were there all the time, but it was only when the servant's spiritual eyes were opened that he was actually able to perceive them.

A number of years ago, during a very difficult season in our lives and ministry, I was crying out to God for a fresh touch of His power and anointing.

While on vacation, we visited Christian Fellowship Church in Belfast. Running a few minutes late, we slipped quietly into the large congregation. That particular Sunday, the church's founding pastor, Paul Reid, was preaching about generations and fresh anointings and mantles for every stage of life's journey. He broke life down into different decades and at the end of each section, he asked people currently in that decade of life to stand for prayer. I was 39 at the time, so I stood with the group aged between 30 and 40. As Paul prayed, something supernatural happened. I literally felt as if a spiritual cloak dropped from Heaven and landed on me. It was an incredibly profound and personal experience. At the end of Paul's prayer, I sat down, somewhat shaken, trying to make sense of what had just happened. All I could think of was the verse where Jesus told his disciples that they would be 'clothed with power from on high'. (Luke 24: 49)

Towards the conclusion of the service, Paul asked the prayer ministry team from the church to come forward. One of the team, a man in his 60's, started walking towards the front but stopped beside me. He leaned across and said these words:

"I saw what happened to you when Paul prayed."

Amazed, I responded, "What did you see?"

"I saw a garment come down from Heaven and land on you."

Still stunned, I mumbled something along the lines of, "I felt something happening. I felt something land on me."

The man looked me in the eyes and said, "I saw exactly what happened. God put a new mantle on you. Don't you ever doubt it. I saw it as clearly as can be."

There were around 400 people in the service that day, but only one was given the spiritual sight to see the invisible world superimposed on the physical room.

We must understand that the line between the seen and unseen realm is very thin. Heaven is not 'up there'. Heaven is all around us. The invisible, spiritual world is just as real and the physical, visible world we can see and touch. When we are born again, our spirits come alive and we become awakened and sensitive to that dimension. For some people who are perhaps more logical in how they think, that will involve hearing from God in a more audible way. For others who are more creative and imaginative, that may well involve seeing images, pictures, visions, and dreams. They are not mutually exclusive and I long for a greater measure of both in my own life. I pray that you do too.

With that in mind, our practical exercise today is a prayer of activation that God would open our eyes to the seer realm. Would you join me?

Practical Exercise:

Place your hands in front of your eyes.

Pray these words:

Father, I thank you that in Christ I am spiritually alive.

Please open my eyes to the unseen realm. Give me a spirit of wisdom and revelation.

Let me see what You are doing in the world around me so that I may join You in advancing Your Kingdom.

Help me to be a blessing and encouragement to others through what you show me.

Thank you for all you are going to reveal to me.

By faith, I now receive all of the spiritual blessings you have provided for me.

In Jesus' powerful name I pray, Amen.

DAY 11

HOW GOD SPEAKS: DREAMS // PART 1

"When we're asleep, God has the opportunity to communicate with us outside of our logical understanding of time and space. He has wisdom to impart to us. But He has to bypass our lower logic to communicate His higher logic. And when we dream, He has a captive audience."
(John Paul Jackson)

I walked into our church building, along with a group of friends. However, inside didn't look at all like a church. It resembled a chaotic neonatal ward. There were new-born babies everywhere, safely enclosed in see-through plastic cots. Some were crying, others lay sound asleep. Strangely, the cots seemed to be arranged in a huge circle, and our beds were in the center of this circle. We were forced to squeeze through and even climb over the cots to get to the place where we were going to rest for the night. I was feeling exhausted and a bit overwhelmed. Eventually, I made it to my bed and was about to clean my teeth using the little sink next to it. However, I found the sink was splattered with baby poo. It stank. I was so annoyed and disgusted. I looked around at my friends, and their sinks were all in the same condition. They were as appalled as I was. However, as we stared at each other in disbelief, all at once, we started to laugh. Not a little chuckle, but a deep belly laugh as if we were having the best time of our lives.

Then I woke up.

This dream took place in late 2011, just a few months after Becky and I had moved to inner-city Dublin to lead a church that had been through a very difficult season and had lost many members.

As soon as I woke up, I immediately knew this dream was from God. How did I know? I'll get to that later.

More importantly, what did the dream mean?

I asked God for the interpretation and this is what I sensed Him say:

"I am going to give you lots and lots of new spiritual babies. You're going to see many people come to faith in Jesus. It's going to be really hard work and it's going to be very messy. But in the middle of it all, it's going to be so much fun. There will be mess in my house, but there is also going to be so much laughter and joy in my house."

And that is exactly what happened. Over the next five years, we saw hundreds of people receive Christ as their Lord and Savior.

Many were from very difficult backgrounds. Some were heroin addicts, prisoners, gangsters, murderers, occultists, Muslims, people with significant mental health issues, and homeless men and women. At one stage, we had a small group made up solely of heroin addicts. We ran an Alpha course in a prison for sex offenders, attended by 15% of the prison population, as well as some of the wardens.

At times, it was very messy. It was exhausting. But there was also so much fun, laughter and fulfillment as we saw lives radically transformed by the Holy Spirit.

THE GOD WHO SPEAKS THROUGH DREAMS

Everybody dreams, every night. In fact, the average person has three to six dreams each night. These most commonly happen in a two-hour time period when our sleep is deepest known as REM or rapid eye movement. In the vast majority of cases, we wake up in the morning and think nothing of what have dreamt about.

However, some dreams are more meaningful and significant than others. It could be that the dream frightens us and so we wake up grateful that it wasn't real. In other cases, we are sorely disappointed that it was in fact a dream.

All through the Bible, we see that one of God's favorite ways to communicate is through dreams, not only with His friends but also to those who don't know Him. In Job 33: 14-15 we read:

"For God does speak - now one way, now another -
though no one perceives it.
In a dream, in a vision of the night,
when deep sleep falls on people
as they slumber in their beds…"

In one sense, we could say that dreams are like prophetic visions, only they happen in our sleep.

Some dreams are literal. What you dream is exactly what is going to happen. However, most often, dreams are communicated in symbolic language, allegories and metaphors, and therefore need to be processed and interpreted.

We see both in Scripture.

In Genesis 31: 11-13 we read:

"The angel of God said to me in the dream, "Jacob." I answered, "Here I am." And he said, "…. Now leave this land at once and go back to your native land."

There was little requirement for Jacob to interpret this dream. It was clear and direct. God was telling Jacob to return home.

When we look at the life of Joseph in the book of Genesis, we see dreams that required more interpretation. For example, as a teenager, Joseph himself had two symbolic dreams:

"Joseph had a dream….He said to them, 'Listen to this dream I had: we were binding sheaves of corn out in the field when suddenly my sheaf rose and stood upright, while your sheaves gathered round mine and bowed down to it.'

His brothers said to him, 'Do you intend to reign over us? Will you actually rule us?' And they hated him all the more because of his dream and what he had said.

Then he had another dream, and he told it to his brothers. 'Listen,' he said, 'I had another dream, and this time the sun and moon and eleven stars were bowing down to me.'"

(Genesis 37: 5-9)

While Joseph's dreams were both different, one clearly confirmed the other.

Why would God give this young man two vivid dreams that would evidently get him into so much trouble with his family?

Firstly, Joseph was not obliged to tell his brothers about his dreams. It didn't take a genius to work out their meaning! At this stage of his life, there was a spirit of pride in his life which would be broken in the years to come. He lacked the wisdom and maturity to properly steward the prophetic revelation. That is something we will look at later in this book. Not everything God shows you is to be shared with everyone!

Secondly, however, I also believe God gave Joseph two similar dreams because he would need to look back at this clear prophetic revelation in the years ahead. Over the next 13 years, Joseph's life was a roller coaster of extreme highs and lows. He was sold by his brothers into slavery. Then later, when things were looking up, he was falsely accused of sexual assault and imprisoned by Pharaoh. As I said in a previous chapter, very often, the clearer the vision, the more difficult the assignment. God knows we will need something unmistakeable to hold onto as we pass through the opposition and trials.

So, some dreams are literal and require little interpretation, while others are more symbolic and need to be processed to figure out what God is communicating. Within both categories, there are four main types of dreams.

PREDICTIVE DREAMS

These are dreams where God is showing the dreamer what is going to happen at some stage in the future. The dream could relate to you personally, it could be for someone else, or it may even be connected to a much wider group of people.

For example, Joseph's first predictive dreams were about his own life. Later, we find him interpreting the dreams of others. Initially, there were the dreams of the cupbearer and the baker. Then later, Pharaoh had two separate prophetic dreams:

"When two full years had passed, Pharaoh had a dream: he was standing by the Nile, when out of the river there came up seven cows, sleek and fat, and they grazed among the reeds. After them, seven other cows, ugly and gaunt, came up out of the Nile and stood beside those on the river-bank. And the cows that were ugly and gaunt ate up the seven sleek, fat cows. Then Pharaoh woke up.

He fell asleep again and had a second dream: seven ears of corn, healthy and good, were growing on a single stalk. After them, seven other ears of corn sprouted – thin and scorched by the east wind. The thin ears of corn swallowed up the seven healthy, full ears. Then Pharaoh woke up; it had been a dream."

(Genesis 41: 1-7)

We are told that none of the magicians or wise men of Egypt could interpret these dreams for the King. However, Joseph is given supernatural wisdom to be able to reveal to Pharaoh that these dreams both mean there will be seven years of abundance followed by seven years of famine.

This is exactly what took place and Joseph was elevated to a position of great authority.

The dream I described at the beginning of this chapter was predictive. We saw many spiritual 'births' and it was messy but also a lot of fun.

We will discuss this more in the next chapter, but as a general rule, if the main character in the dream is you, it is most likely to be about your own life and future.

WARNING DREAMS

These are dreams where God is seeking to protect you or others from some current situation or forthcoming incident. These types of dreams tend to be much more vivid and direct. Ambiguity in a warning dream isn't very helpful.

After the birth of Jesus, in Matthew 2: 13 we read:

"...an angel of the Lord appeared to Joseph in a dream. 'Get up,' he said, 'take the child and his mother and escape to Egypt. Stay there until I tell you, for Herod is going to search for the child to kill him.'"

This was a very direct warning with clear instructions because the stakes were so high. There was no interpretation required.

In his book *Confessions of a Reformission Rev.*, Pastor Mark Driscoll describes a warning dream he had in the early years of church planting in Seattle. A seasoned older pastor with much ministry experience had arrived at the church and had become somewhat of a mentor to the young pastor. Over time, the older man began to seek a position of leadership. Seeking discernment, Pastor Driscoll asked the Lord to show him what to do. He writes what happened next:

"I had never had a prophetic dream. I actually was not sure that such miraculous things still happened and was skeptical of prophetic dreams altogether. But while I was sleeping one night, the Holy Spirit gave me a dream in which I was standing in the foyer of our rented church on the opening night of our church plant. As I turned around in my dream, the older man walked in by himself, carrying a Bible in a brown leather case and wearing a blue shirt, green shorts, sandals, and a homemade cross around his neck. He informed me that he wanted to pastor the church and

that I should step aside and let him. God then spoke Acts 20:28 – 31 to me, saying, "Keep watch over yourselves and all the flock of which the Holy Spirit has made you overseers. Be shepherds of the church of God, which he bought with his own blood. I know that after I leave, savage wolves will come in among you and will not spare the flock. Even from your own number men will arise and distort the truth in order to draw away disciples after them. So be on your guard!"...

....I then woke up to tell my wife that God had revealed to me that the older man was a wolf sent by Satan and that Jesus wanted me to protect and lead the small flock he had given me. We prayed together.

On the opening night of our church plant, the service was just getting started when my wife realized that she had forgotten her Bible in the foyer. I jumped up to get it, and as I turned around, I found myself standing alone in the foyer, just as I had been in my dream. The older man then walked in the door wearing the same outfit he had worn in the dream and came toward me speaking every word he had in my dream. I was so stunned that I was momentarily speechless. When I collected my thoughts, I told him to leave our church and never come back.

A few months later, another older pastor contacted me and said that the man God warned me of had been kicked out of his denomination on suspicion of undermining young pastors and taking money from young churches.

....Since that time, I have had many other similar dreams and words from God and always know they are from God because they come true and are confirmed by God with Scripture."

Obviously, not every dream is from God, and not every negative dream about something or someone is a warning dream. You may be prone to nightmares which is an entirely different subject in itself. Very often our dreams will correlate with what is going on in our waking lives. For example, if something is on your mind all day, there is a good chance that your mind will continue to process it while you sleep.

However, God does use dreams to protect His children from harm and deception. It could be about something as ordinary as buying a house or a relationship. Author and speaker, Perry Stone, relates one such dream:

"I was eighteen years of age, traveling from church to church conducting weekly revivals. At one location, a family I knew with a daughter about my age wanted me to go out with her to eat. My policy was to only go out with a group of young people and avoid going out alone with the opposite sex. Soon she began to speak to friends that she was serious about me and thought our friendship could lead to eventual marriage. At the same time, I dreamed that she was pregnant. In the dream, the Lord told me to avoid her...

I sent word to her through a friend not to have any contact with me again. One month later it was confirmed that she was pregnant, and she married the father of the child shortly thereafter."

Often, a warning dream will be confirming something you already sense in your spirit or it will be confirmed by other people or circumstances. When God gives you a clear warning dream, you ignore it at your peril. He is trying to keep you from a lot of hurt and heartache.

SOUL DREAMS

These are dreams that reveal events, concerns, emotions, or feelings that we are struggling to process or trying to repress. Ecclesiastes 5: 3 says:

*"For a dream comes through much **activity**..."* (NKJV)
*"For the dream comes through much **effort**..."* (AMP)
*"For a dream comes with much **business**..."* (ESV)
*"A dream comes when there are many **cares**..."* (NIV)

Each translation is telling us that a dream can often relate to our daily activities and cares. When waking from a dream it is helpful to look back on the events of the past few days that may have triggered a soul dream. You may be anxious about something - perhaps there has been an element of stress or tension you need to give attention to. You may be looking forward to an event, which your dream may be connected to.

A few years ago, I repeatedly had the exact same dream. In it, I was incredibly thirsty. However, no matter how much water I drank, the thirst couldn't be quenched. I would wake up thinking I must need a drink, when in fact, in the natural, I felt completely fine.

As I prayed into it, I discerned that the dream was pointing to a significant lack of satisfaction in my life and ministry at the time that I had been trying to ignore. I thought that if I kept busy, a sense of fulfillment would return. However, I was simply feeling more and more empty. It's interesting that these dreams stopped a few years ago when I began Daily Prophetic and writing books. Evidently, a sense of satisfaction and fulfillment had returned.

Not long ago, I had another recurring dream in which I was walking into an exam hall with a frightening realization that I was totally unprepared for the test I was about to take. I hadn't studied the subject and knew that I was going to fail. I believe God was showing me that there are desires in my heart and places He wanted to take me, but that I wasn't yet ready. I needed to discipline myself and submit more fully to His preparation process.

Sometimes actual memories resurface in your dreams. People and events from the past may appear. This could be a sign that there were situations that weren't fully resolved or that you need to take some time to properly process a relational breakdown. As Zoran Paunovich says:

"What you fail to confront during the day often confronts you during the night…. A dream does not disguise emotion. Your feelings are a true and honest reflection of the actual condition of your soul. Feelings expressed in a dream can help you identify and deal with any unresolved conflict, guilt, grief, anxiety, anger, tension etc…."

SPIRITUAL WARFARE DREAMS

These are similar to warning dreams, but most often happen at times of current or upcoming spiritual attack. In the dream, you might actually be fighting against someone or something.

Recently, two nights in a row, I had dreams in which I was fighting with another person I didn't recognize. The altercations were so vivid that in both dreams, I actually physically kicked out in bed, on one occasion making contact with my wife. She wasn't impressed! Evidently, God was warning me of spiritual attacks and I took extra time each day to pray for protection over every aspect of my life.

God may use a dream to reveal the presence, plans, or strategy of the enemy. At other times, you may even encounter a demon in a dream.

As with any other dream, seek to ascertain the source and cause of it. Is there something happening in your life at the moment which could be used by the enemy to inflict harm on you? Are you experiencing unusual opposition or adversity? Have you been struggling with a particular sin or weakness? Is there someone who has come into your life recently that you have a bad feeling about?

While such dreams are disturbing, we do not need to be afraid.

Firstly, God is revealing the schemes of the enemy to you because He wants you to stand firm and resist the attack.

Secondly, you have been given spiritual authority in Christ to overcome every demonic assignment and affliction.

Pray for discernment. Ask God to make clear what He is showing you in the dream.

If you know there is an area of unrepentant sin in your life, deal with it. Take it to the cross.

If necessary, break any agreement you might have made with the enemy. Have others pray with you also.

Also, find out if there anything in your home which could have a demonic presence attached to it? It's amazing how seemingly harmless ornaments or souvenirs bought overseas can have dark spiritual forces attached to them.

Take whatever action is necessary to remove anything which could be hindering you in your walk with the Lord.

NIGHTMARES

This is also an appropriate place to mention nightmares. These can have many causes, some spiritual, some natural. They can be related to significant events in our past or simply connected to what we watched on TV before we went to bed.

Helen Calder says this:

"Repeated nightmares can be a sign of having an 'open doorway' in our lives for demonic oppression. Those who have experienced trauma, or been involved in the occult (personally or generationally), for example, may be vulnerable in this area. But bad dreams and nightmares can be redeemed and overcome."

Other people suffer from sleep paralysis. You wake up terrified but literally can't move. This can especially affect teenagers.

Again, it is important to examine what else is going on in your life. Pray and ask the Lord to reveal anything that could be causing such a response. Take authority over any spirit which could be afflicting you and command it to leave. Submit your mind and dream life to the Holy Spirit. Before you go to sleep, fill your mind with the Word of God.

For many years, my wife had recurrent nightmares. In the early years of our marriage, almost every night, I would be awakened by her screaming. Sometimes this happened two or three times in one night. Many of these dreams involved snakes crawling over her and other terrifying situations.

Eventually, Becky signed up for a *Sozo* session at a local church. *Sozo* is an inner healing and deliverance ministry that originated at Bethel Church in Redding, California (http://bethelsozo.com/). While I don't know exactly what happened in my wife's Sozo session, I am sure of two things: (i) For three days afterward she was completely exhausted. It was as if she had run a marathon. Clearly, a deeply spiritual and physical encounter had taken place; (ii) Since then, she has very rarely ever experienced nightmares like those she had before. Something had been broken off from her and deep healing had taken place.

Of course, she is still very careful about what she watches on TV or allows into her mind. I love gritty British crime dramas. Becky finds that these can affect her dreams and so she avoids them. You too may have to cut some things out of your life which aren't necessarily bad in themselves, but they are affecting and afflicting you.

In the next chapter, we'll continue to explore different types of dreams and also focus on how we interpret what God is revealing to us as we sleep.

Let me finish today by saying this: while we all dream every night, **when you do have a significant prophetic dream, you will usually wake up immediately after it with a very strong sense that there was something different about that dream.** I have found this to be true in my own life and many others have told me the same. You awaken and you just *know* that God was getting your attention. That is why it is so important to complete today's practical exercise.

Practical Exercise: Keep a notebook and pen beside your bed. Each morning, or if you happen to wake up during the night, jot down the details of any dreams that you can remember.

Obviously, some will be more significant than others. But keep a record of them.

Over time, you may find that certain dreams are recurring or that God is highlighting particular aspects of dreams.

Pray into these and ask Him to help you interpret and understand what He is communicating to you.

Perhaps even share them with a close friend or mature believer. You might be amazed at some patterns you would have missed if you hadn't journaled what God was showing you in your sleep.

DAY 12
HOW GOD SPEAKS: DREAMS // PART 2

"From the beginning, the two primary ways the Lord has spoken to his people have been through dreams and visions… however, this is probably one of the least understood subjects in the church. As we come to the end of this age, it will become increasingly essential for us to know how to distinguish dreams and visions that are from the Lord from those that are not. We must also know how to interpret them."

(Rick Joyner)

The soft-spoken lady in her 50's sat in my office and explained an unusual dream which had now recurred three times. I don't remember all of the details, but it involved birds and nests and locked doors and clocks. It was so random. I recall thinking, 'I don't have a clue what this means.' However, as her pastor, I thought I'd better try to help as she was clearly troubled and convinced that these dreams were from God.

I suggested we pray. I asked the Holy Spirit for the gift of interpretation and that He would reveal what this dream meant. Honestly, I wasn't feeling particularly hopeful as I'd never interpreted a dream in my life, never mind one as obscure as this.

However, in the moments that followed, even I was shocked by the words that came out of my mouth. I broke the dream down into different parts and explained what each part meant. I then interpreted it as meaning that God was going to heal her relationship with her sister from whom she had become increasingly estranged over the years. However, she wasn't to initiate or force a reconciliation, that would only push her sister further away. Instead, she was to give her sister much more space than before, and soon, through various circumstances, the two of them would be reunited.

While she was thankful for the interpretation, she admitted that she would struggle to implement it. By nature, she was someone who liked to fix things. She also liked to be in control. To let go and create more space in the relationship was going to take some discipline.

Six months later, she and her sister had started building bridges. While by no means best friends, they were communicating and seeking to heal old wounds. The lady from my church told me this: "My sister said that it was only because I gave her space that she decided to contact me. The distance made her realize that she missed me. In fact, back when I had my dream, she apparently had decided that if I tried to force more contact or push for reconciliation, that she was going to cut me out of her life completely."

Isn't our God so good? Think about it. How incredible is it that the Creator of Heaven and earth would care about the relationship between two sisters so much that he would inspire prophetic dreams and then give me a supernatural ability, at that moment, to interpret them?

However, I do have to wonder: why does God speak so often through complex imagery and symbols? Would it not be easier for everyone if He were to communicate in dreams more clearly and directly?

Of course, sometimes He does. Occasionally the meaning of the dream is plain and literal. What you see correlates exactly with what God is saying. But most of the time, dreams take some unravelling and interpretation.

HIDE AND SEEK

Proverbs 25: 2 says:

"It is the glory of God to conceal things, but the glory of kings is to search things out."

When we were kids, my parents would try so hard to hide birthday and Christmas gifts from my brother and I. It became my personal mission to find out where they were stashed. Dad and mum became more and more creative in their hiding places (the attic or the neighbor's shed) and I became more and more determined in my search. It developed into a challenge to see who would win the game of 'gift hide-and-seek'.

The thing is, even though the present was hidden for a while, my parents always intended that I would receive it. Using a similar metaphor, Bill Johnson says this about why God speaks through symbols and imagery:

"People wonder why God doesn't always speak in more open terms – audibly, with visible signs, etc. I don't know how or why it works this way, but the Bible indicates that God receives more glory when He conceals, rather than making things obvious. It is more glorious for Him to hide, and have us seek....

Revelation always brings responsibility, and hunger is the thing that prepares our hearts to carry the weight of that responsibility. By keeping revelation from those without hunger, God actually protects them from certain failure to carry the responsibility it would lay on them. And so He conceals. Yet, He doesn't conceal from us; He conceals for us!"

I love that. God doesn't hide things *from* us, so much as he hides them *for* us.

Bill Johnson goes on to say:

"Our royal identity never shines brighter than when we pursue hidden things with the confidence that we have legal access to such things. Mysteries are our inheritance. Our kingship, our role in ruling and reigning with Christ, comes to the forefront when we seek Him for answers to the dilemmas of the world around us."

So, God's glory is somehow magnified by making us search for meaning and our glory as His sons and daughters is revealed in pursuing an understanding and interpretation of His mysteries!

Similarly, Jesus very often taught the crowds using parables, stories of varying complexity that required the hearer to really listen and interpret the meaning for themselves. In Matthew 13 we read:

"The disciples came to him and asked, "Why do you speak to the people in parables?"

He replied, "Because the knowledge of the secrets of the kingdom of heaven has been given to you, but not to them."

(vv 10-11)

As believers, God has uniquely privileged us with access to His secrets and mysteries. As we hunger for increased intimacy with the Father and search for understanding of His will, He loves to supernaturally reveal His plans, purposes, desires and designs for our lives and this world.

Dreams aren't given to keep us in the dark but to awaken us to the 'more' that is available to us as our inheritance in Christ. They are an invitation to begin an exploration through prayer and understanding God's ways.

Something else to bear in mind is that, while the enemy can influence our dream life, he can't access the dreams that come from the Father. By speaking to us as we sleep, God can hide His plans and secrets from the demonic spiritual realm. That is why He instructed Joseph and Mary in a dream to flee to Egypt with Jesus. The instruction was hidden and protected because it was sealed by the dream.

It should be clear, therefore, that interpreting dreams (as well as visions and other modes of revelation) will take discipline and cultivation and pursuit. But it is something that every believer can do and is so incredibly valuable and worthwhile.

INTERPRETING THE LANGUAGE OF HEAVEN

Every dream from God has mystery and clarity. While the meaning may not be immediately plain to us, the Father knows precisely what He is communicating and revealing. It is our responsibility, in dependence on the Holy Spirit, to interpret what we are being shown.

While some people have a gift of interpreting dreams, every believer can grow and develop in learning the language of the Holy Spirit. As I've already made clear, the Father loves to reveal mysteries to all His children.

Also, it is important to remember that the goal when interpreting a dream for someone else is not to look impressive but to unlock wisdom and release destiny.

With all of that in mind, let's look at some principles of dream interpretation.

Interpretation always begins with total dependence on God. When faced with interpreting the dream of King Nebuchadnezzar, Daniel made it very clear that "No wise man, enchanter, magician or diviner can explain to the king the mystery he has asked about, but there is a God in heaven who reveals mysteries." (Daniel 2: 27-28)

While we can learn what various symbols and images typically mean, dream interpretation is a supernaturally empowered ability, given by the Holy Spirit. Therefore, our posture is always one of humility and teachability. While God will always give the interpretation at some point, it could happen immediately or at some time in the future. The key is to keep seeking His face and pursuing His heart.

Like any language, interpretation deals in vocabulary. When it comes to interpreting dreams, we need to have some understanding of:

(i) Biblical vocabulary: what does this number, symbol, image, etc. mean in the Scriptures?

Some symbols are consistent all throughout Scripture. For example, feet generally represent territory or your direction in life. Wine represents joy or the Holy Spirit. Gold represents kingship, wealth, and value.

As we grow in our knowledge of the Bible, we will find it much easier to interpret many facets of dreams.

(ii) Personal vocabulary: what does this person, place, symbol, represent to you?

Our personal vocabulary comes from our life experiences, as well as our personality traits and idiosyncrasies. For example, if you hate dogs, a dream with a dog will mean something very different to you than it will to someone who adores these four-legged creatures.

Most of your dreams will be related to you in some way. Even when you see other people in your dream, God is generally speaking to you about your own sphere of influence. This would include your relationships, finances, job, hobbies, family, and ministry. I am more likely to have dreams about the church I lead than someone who has no leadership position or responsibility. As the Lord opens up your sphere of influence and widens the territory in which He has given you authority, your dream life will often begin to match that.

Everybody can acquire the basic skills of interpretation. With learning, practice and experience, you can grow in your understanding of what various symbols and images mean.

Generally, some dreams mean the same thing every time. Take my own example in the previous chapter of not being prepared for an exam. A dream in which you are taking a test will almost always mean that there is a season of promotion coming. The Lord is wanting to train, mature and develop you. Therefore, you will keep repeating the test until you pass. If you are repeatedly having this dream it simply means that you are not yet ready. Don't be discouraged. The Lord is determined to get you there!

A dream can have more than one meaning. Just like the parables of Jesus, there may be several layers of interpretation. Just because one meaning seems immediately obvious, don't assume that there isn't some deeper revelation that the Lord wants to show you.

You might not always know whether the dream is literal or symbolic. For example, imagine you had a dream where you were sitting in a room with the President or Queen. Does this mean that one day you will actually meet this person at some stage in the future? Or does it mean that God is releasing increased governmental influence and authority into your life? Or perhaps both? God will either make it clear or time will tell.

DREAM DIAGNOSIS

It doesn't matter if the dream was personal or you are interpreting it for someone else, here are some good questions to help you explore and discern its meaning:

Where did the dream come from? What was the source?

(i) Is it my own mind and emotions processing current events? For example, am I currently under stress? Is my life too busy or too fast?

(ii) Could it be deceiving spirits? Typically this will relate to dreams bringing a sense of fear, dread, or panic. The Bible tells us clearly that God is love and that His perfect love casts out all fear. Therefore, any revelation from the Father will never carry fear, except for a holy reverence of the Lord.

Nightmares fall into this category. As I said in the last chapter, these could be from the enemy or from media you are consuming i.e. TV shows, video games, etc.

Other types of dreams originating with the enemy include dreams of deception designed to create images and impressions that turn us away from God and dark dreams i.e. dreams that are somber, depressing, grey. Again, the Bible tells us that God is light and in Him there is no darkness at all.

(iii) Dreams from the Father designed to release destiny.

These are dreams which bring prophetic revelation of God's good future for you or a warning intended to help you protect what He has already entrusted to you.

What was going on in your life when you had the dream?

Are there any significant events or life transitions taking place? e.g. moving house, getting married, changing jobs, relational issues. Thoughts about these will obviously seep from your waking life into your dream life.

Are you observing in the dream looking from an outside perspective or are you an active participant in the dream?

If you are a bystander watching events unfold, that is an indicator that the dream may not be about you. If you are the main focus and character in the dream, it most likely is about you.

What do the other people in the dream represent to you?

If you see your father in the dream, how you interpret it will obviously depend on the relationship you have (or had) with him. If your dream involves someone from your past who did you great wrong, they are very likely to be a symbol of betrayal or danger.

Where there any words used in the dream?

Obviously, the words spoken, as well as who said them and how they were said, will be significant in your interpretation process.

What emotions were connected to the dream?

Did you feel a sense of joy, peace, or excitement as you were dreaming? Or was there fear, anxiety, or apprehension?

How did you feel when you woke up?

Was there a sense of relief, concern, confusion, expectation?

If you are having night terrors, is there any open door where the enemy has been given the legal access?

This may or may not involve personal sin issues in your life. Unforgiveness is one very common doorway for the enemy to gain a foothold. Sexual impurity is another.

On the other hand, it could be through something that happened to you, over which you had no control. For example, serious accidents or sudden losses may result in a spirit of trauma attaching itself to your life. Past abuse, be that physical, sexual, or emotional, is another obvious way the enemy seeks to gain a presence in our minds and bodies.

Understanding these events can help you to process and interpret what is happening in dreams. In some cases, there may need to be counselling, emotional healing or deliverance before complete freedom is experienced.

In the next chapter, we will look further at how we interpret specific aspects of dreams. This will be helpful also for interpreting visions, pictures and other prophetic revelation.

As I conclude this chapter, let me leave you with a few important reminders.

While God does speak through dreams, not every dream is from God. Don't become obsessed with over-analyzing every dream. When the Father is clearly speaking, you will know it and He will reinforce it.

Don't change your life because of a dream. I would always counsel people to avoid making significant decisions based on any one supernatural experience, whether that be a dream, vision or prophetic word. The more important the decision, the more frequently and clearly the Lord will confirm it to you.

Seek help from people who you know are gifted in dream interpretation. This is especially true as you are growing in your own ability to interpret dreams. Find someone who can break down the various components of dreams and see how they process the different symbols, words and pictures. If you don't know anyone personally, there are some good videos online of leaders like the late John Paul Jackson taking people through their dreams and explaining what they mean.

Some dreams can only be fully processed and understood in the future. As much as you pray and seek discernment, the interpretation of the dream may be hidden from you until a later time. Then, perhaps something will happen in your life, and it will just 'click'. The pieces all fall into place and you can see what God has been saying.

Practical Exercise: Watch the following videos of John Paul Jackson interpreting various dreams. Of course, you might not agree with everything he says. But it will help you to see how he breaks each aspect of the dream down and seeks to bring Divine wisdom into some very unusual symbols and images.

Dream Interpretation - John Paul Jackson - Parts 1-9
https://www.youtube.com/playlist?list=PLBF1050B056E908AC

DAY 13

HOW GOD SPEAKS: DREAMS // PART 3

"Understanding how God speaks at night is pivotal in our spiritual growth. Being fluent in the language in which someone is speaking to us obviously has profound implications on our ability to communicate effectively and build a closer relationship with that person. By learning God's heart language of dreams we demonstrate our commitment and desire for deeper intimacy with Him. Becoming proficient in interpreting His visions of the night is a game-changer in our walk with the Lord."

(Dr. Charity Kayembe)

In 2020, during the first ten weeks of lockdown, I took our church through 50 daily studies in the book of Revelation. If you've ever studied this apocalyptic book, you will know that the first five chapters are reasonably straightforward. The Apostle John has a vision of Jesus, he receives seven letters for churches in Asia, and then He sees God exalted, high and holy, upon his throne. Then it starts to get strange. And much more difficult to interpret. You start reading about seven seals and seven trumpets and seven bowls. Then a beast and a dragon appear, followed by a prostitute called Babylon. I began to understand why so many pastors stop preaching this book at chapter six! However, as I persevered through it, I discovered that the puzzle pieces started to fit together. Again and again, when I was faced with a symbolic image or number, I found myself saying: "I've seen this earlier in the book somewhere." And, by going back and seeing what it meant the last time, I was much easier able to decipher what it was relating to in its current context.

Dreams are very similar to the book of Revelation. Full of images, symbols and metaphors, it's easy to be completely overwhelmed and simply give up on even trying to interpret our own, or others, dreams. However, if we will stick with them, we will soon discover that, like a jigsaw puzzle, the pieces do start to fit together. Common themes and images appear and begin to make more sense. Or, to use another analogy, you begin to learn the vocabulary of dream language. Words that you never understood before keep reappearing and you now know how to interpret them with much more ease.

We have already seen that generally, dreams fall into three main categories:

A simple message dream: For example, the warning that Joseph received in Matthew 2 about escaping to Egypt. This dream was clear and straightforward, requiring little interpretation.

A simple symbolic dream: While these are slightly less direct than message dreams, they don't take a lot of interpretation. In Genesis 37, the dream that Joseph had as a teenager about the sun, moon and eleven stars bowing down to him would be an example of a simple symbolic dream. His family all immediately understood what it meant.

A complex symbolic dream: This is the type of dream that requires someone who has the spiritual gift of interpreting dreams or someone who has learned and developed their interpretative skills. I differentiate the two because I have seen both throughout the years. I have a friend who is has a spiritual gift of interpreting dreams. Prophetically he is supernaturally enabled to unravel complex mysteries and make sense of them. I know other people who have studied dream language in a similar way to how I learned to speak French in school. They begin with the most common symbols and, over time, work their way down to learning the nuances and intricacies of the language.

So, if you are just beginning to walk in the realm of dream language, be patient. It will get easier. Also, don't forget, you have a wonderful tutor who will teach and guide you along the path. Jesus has promised supernatural assistance:

"...the Advocate, the Holy Spirit, whom the Father will send in my name, will teach you all things and will remind you of everything I have said to you." (John 14: 26)

"I have much more to say to you, more than you can now bear. But when he, the Spirit of truth, comes, he will guide you into all the truth. He will not speak on his own; he will speak only what he hears, and he will tell you what is yet to come. He will glorify me because it is from me that he will receive what he will make known to you."

(John 16: 12-14)

The Holy Spirit will be your mentor and friend, revealing to you the mysteries of the Father.

With that in mind, let us begin with the basics of dream vocabulary and look at the most common dreams and what they might mean.

THE MOST COMMON DREAMS

HOUSES: It has been said that around 40% of dreams involve houses. A house normally represents your life. However, you will want to ask:

Is it old or new? Is it where you currently live or a house you grew up in?

Is it small or large? What color is it?

It is run down or in good condition?

Where are you in the house? The kitchen, the bedroom, the attic?

Individual rooms may represent different things. For example, the bedroom often relates to issues of intimacy. The bathroom represents cleansing. The family room represents your closest relationships.

TRANSPORTATION: When you dream about a vehicle, it normally represents the calling you have on your life or the direction you are travelling. Cars, planes, buses, etc. may be symbols of the type or even the size of the vocation you are engaged in. Some questions to ask are:

What color is the vehicle?

What make or model is it?

Who is driving it? Where are you located inside it?

What speed was it travelling at?

Is the journey smooth or rough?

In my book *SPIRIT SPEAK*, I share about a dream I had while on vacation a few years ago. The part of the dream which was most vivid was that I was a driver of a double-decker (two storey) bus. However, when I mounted the bus to start driving, my seat was located on the upper deck and a few rows from the front. It was totally the wrong position for driving. In the dream, I remember saying: "I can't see anything. I'm not sure where I'm going." I started to move forward anyway, trying to sense where I was meant to be, but it was frightening and dangerous.

At that time in my life, I was struggling to find vision or direction for the church I was leading. The bus represented the church. As the leader, I was in charge of driving the vehicle. However, I wasn't in a position where I could clearly see the road ahead. To be effective in moving forward, I would have to make some adjustments.

SCHOOL/TESTS: I have already mentioned my own dreams about tests in an earlier chapter. When you dream about school it normally represents that the Lord is in the process of training and developing you. A test normally means that He wants to advance or promote you.

CLOTHES: Different types of clothing represent different aspects of your life. For example, work clothes relate to your job or career. Pyjamas will correlate with your home life. So if you have a dream in which you show up to work in your pyjamas, that could represent that your home life is affecting your work life.
If you dream that you are wearing an expensive gown, that could indicate that the Lord wants you to see yourself as having greater value than you currently give yourself credit for.

If you are wearing clothes that don't fit, it could mean that you've outgrown a realm in your life or there is a new assignment ahead that the Lord wants you to grow into.

What about dreams in which you are naked? These could indicate that you feel vulnerable, exposed or fearful in a particular situation. Perhaps greater transparency is required in a particular area of your life. These types of dreams can often occur during period of significant transition where you are 'taking off' an old identity and dressing for your new role, position or location.

PREGNANT: Many people, even men, have had dreams in which they are pregnant. While, for a female, occasionally this dream can be literal, most often it signifies that a new season of purpose or destiny is being birthed in your life.
How far on are you in the pregnancy? If you are actually giving birth, it means that you should expect change imminently.

WEDDINGS: These dreams can cause much confusion and even heartache. I have heard from individuals who had vivid dreams in which they were marrying someone they knew. In some cases, they were thrilled as they were genuinely very attracted to this person. In other cases, they were horrified. He or she was not their type at all!

If you are in a relationship and you dream about your wedding with this person, ask yourself: how did I feel? Were you excited? Or were you anxious or apprehensive? The Lord could be revealing some things about the relationship that you haven't wanted to admit to yourself (or your significant other).

A wedding can also speak of a union or partnership. It may represent the coming together of an idea, project, or dream. Divorce, on the other hand, can speak of division, separation, disharmony and disagreement.

PEOPLE: When you dream about a person, don't automatically assume that the dream directly relates to them. Remember that most of your dreams are about you. Instead, ask yourself: what does this person represent in my life? When I think about them, what is the first quality that comes to mind? What emotions do I feel about this individual?

For example, if the person is arrogant or dogmatic, could the Lord be gently telling you that you might want to be a little more humble or flexible in an area of your life? If they are fun-loving and spontaneous, maybe you are being encouraged to relax more and take life a little less seriously.

If you dream about someone with whom you once had a relationship, don't jump to the conclusion that God wants you to get back together. This kind of dream may indicate that you are in danger of falling back into old ways and patterns of thinking. Or it could be a warning that someone currently in your life has similar traits to that person from your past. Again, the key is to ask yourself what that person represents to you – good or bad.

ANIMALS: Different animals symbolize certain emotions, characteristics, attitude and attributes. The key question again is: what does this animal represent *to me*? For example, some people love cats and so a dream about one of these feline creatures might represent joy or companionship. I don't like cates at all. In fact, I'm highly allergic to them. So a dream about a cat may represent a risk or an irritant to me.

Generally, animals such as lions and horses represent boldness, fortitude and strength. Rats and pigs represent something unclean. Birds often symbolize freedom and unrestricted flight. Snakes are perhaps the most common of all animal dreams. Dreams with snakes most often represent the devil and his demonic hosts at work through lying, accusation, attack, etc.

TEETH: It is surprising how many people have dreams about the condition of their teeth. Wisdom teeth reveal the need for wisdom. Loose, rotten, or falling out teeth indicate that there are important areas of your life you are neglecting and that urgently need some attention. Shiny, sharp teeth might mean you are experiencing favor in an area of life such as work i.e. you are at the cutting edge.

DYING: Again, a dream in which you see someone die does not generally mean that their demise is imminent. The person is symbolic and represents something that is passing away or departing from your life. For example, I know of someone who dreamt that their best friend had died. Not long after that, they relocated to another country. The dream meant that their relationship, as it had been, was coming to an end.

COLORS: Obviously, there are many variations of colors that could represent hundreds of different things. This could be a whole chapter in itself. However, typically when you think of gold, what comes to mind? Something of value and importance. What about green? It could be new beginnings (green shoots appearing) or, depending on the context, it could be envy. Black generally represents darkness and negativity whereas white symbolizes purity and righteousness. Blue often relates to heaven or the Holy Spirit, whereas red represents danger or bloodshed

NUMBERS: Like colors, numbers are highly symbolic throughout the Bible. Here are a few guidelines for interpreting numbers.

The first use of a number in Scripture generally conveys its spiritual meaning. For example, one means new beginnings, six is the number of man, seven is the number of perfection or completeness.

Multiples of numbers, such as seeing doubles or triples, carry basically the same meaning only they intensify the truth. For example, the mark of the beast in Revelation is 666. He may appear god-like, but he is merely a creature and is far below perfection.

Obviously, this list of common dreams is by no means exhaustive. But hopefully, you are beginning to get some idea of how you might start interpreting dreams. It's also worth noting that these same principles and symbols also relate to prophetic visions and words. You could be praying with someone and see a picture of a gold lion. Or perhaps receive a prophetic word saying: "The Lord is taking you from a small house to a larger castle."

CLOSING THOUGHTS ON DREAMS

It's always best to reduce the dream to its simplest form and work from there. Instead of getting bogged down in the details, ask yourself: what is the main theme here? What was the most prominent action, item, place, emotion? Like a movie, every dream has a theme. Were you running, crying, falling? Was it at home, on a beach, in a prison? Were you happy or angry?

Next, remember that context determines interpretation. What does this item, color, etc. mean in the overall context of the Bible? What is the context of my life at this time? So, again, the key question isn't 'what do I see?' but 'what does that represent to me right now?' Or in the case of another person, what does this represent to them?

Repeated dreams or dreams which are similar, simply mean that the Lord is reinforcing what He is communicating to you because it is important.

As I said at the beginning of this chapter, over time you will develop your own dream vocabulary. A person, object, color, or number will immediately have some significance for you.

Ultimately, though, we always remain fully dependant on the Holy Spirit to guide us into an accurate interpretation of any revelation. While Daniel in the Old Testament was clearly gifted in dream interpretation, he acknowledged that no human could interpret the

King's dream "but there is a God in heaven who reveals mysteries." (Daniel 2: 28)

No matter how proficient you become in the language of dreams, never forget to seek God for the meaning to the mysteries.

Practical Exercise: Over the coming days, start to take note of colors, numbers, people, items, vehicles, etc. and ask yourself: what do these represent? It will be almost like trying out a new language you are learning. Pay attention especially to patterns or repetition. For example, one evening last week, we were surprised by a beautiful butterfly suddenly flying around our living room. The doors and windows were closed and so it seemed to come from nowhere. Then, a few days later, as we were out for lunch, a very similar butterfly came and landed on Becky's arm. A butterfly symbolizes transformation and new beginnings. The Lord has got our attention.

DAY 14

HOW GOD SPEAKS: WORDS OF KNOWLEDGE // PART 1

"Words of knowledge ground you in the truth that God knows you, and He loves you. Hearing His purpose for our lives causes a moment of wonder and awe as we witness the nature of God's love and nurturing care put on display for everyone to see."

(Shawn Bolz)

A word of knowledge is the ability to know something about a person or situation that has been supernaturally revealed by God. It is mentioned by Paul as being one of the revelation gifts of the Spirit in 1 Corinthians 12: 8:

"…for to one is given the word of wisdom through the Spirit, to another **the word of knowledge** through the same Spirit…"

A word of knowledge is often confused as prophecy as they are both similar in many ways. However, a word of knowledge tends to be a more specific piece of information and is therefore short and very precise. It normally comes as a simple impression, thought or physical feeling. Also, a word of knowledge tends to be more related to the past or present, whereas a prophetic revelation speaks from the present into the future.

GOD'S WAY OF POINTING AT PEOPLE

In my experience, a word of knowledge is often used to identify a person or people for further ministry of some kind. For example, a word of knowledge about a particular physical affliction could be used to identify that person to receive prayer for healing.

At the beginning of 2020, I was asked to teach on the prophetic in a church around two hours from my hometown. Following on from my message, we entered into a time of ministry. I had never visited this congregation before which, for me, makes it much easier to minister. I have no prior knowledge of the people or place which might taint or influence any prophetic words I give.

Immediately the Lord impressed a date on my mind: July 8th. That's all I had, July 8th. So, I asked: "Does July 8th means anything to anyone?" A couple seated to my right shouted out that July 8th was their wedding anniversary.

What should I do now? In the past, I would have thought that the date itself was significant. As July 8th was their wedding anniversary, I would have assumed that God wanted to speak into their marriage and relationship. That would make sense, wouldn't it?

However, a few months prior to this, through trial and error, God had taught me some important things about what to do in a situation like this. I had been ministering in another setting and had asked the group of around 50 people if anyone had an identical twin. A lady who was part of our own congregation raised her hand. I was really surprised as I had absolutely no idea that she had a twin sister. I proceeded to try to give a word about her relationship with her sister. After all, that must be why God had given me the revelation about her having a twin, right? However, as I began to speak, inside I could feel the words were falling flat. It felt forced and contrived. The recipient didn't appear particularly moved by anything I was saying either.

I was struggling and becoming increasingly uptight and intense inside. That's the worst thing you can do when you're trying to hear from God. The more relaxed you are, the better.

After a few moments of rambling, I stopped and said: "Let's just wait."

In the silence, I calmed my mind. I went back to basics. The first rule of New Testament prophecy is that it is for strengthening, encouragement and comfort. So, I started to share some very simple words of encouragement over this lady about her faithfulness as a mother. As I spoke, the words began to flow freely. They became more specific and precise. The atmosphere in the room shifted. I shared what I sensed the Lord was doing in the lady's life and where He was leading her in the coming days. Tears filled her eyes. It was clear that God was speaking directly to His beloved daughter. At the end, I was honestly so relieved.

For days after that meeting, I thought about what had happened. How had I got it wrong? And then also, how did I finish up getting it right?

The Lord began to show me that the fact that this lady was a twin was not significant in and of itself. That information (or revelation) was simply a word of knowledge to specifically identify her out of the crowd. How else could she have been selected? It would have to be something unique to her. I took note of what God had taught me, determined to not make that mistake again.

So now, a few months later in a different setting, having discovered that July 8th was this couple's wedding anniversary, I knew not to make too much of that information. All it meant was that God wanted to speak to them together as a couple. After the gathering, I prayed and prophesied privately over them about their future role in the church and where God was leading them in ministry together. Along with their Lead Pastor, they affirmed that what I shared clearly confirmed what they had been already sensing.

SHORT AND SIMPLE

Like I said earlier, a word of knowledge is generally very short and precise. It's a simple piece or fragment of information that God gives to specifically select an individual He wants to minister to. It can also be a key that unlocks the heart of the other person, opening them up to the work of the Holy Spirit. We see this in the interaction Jesus had with a Samaritan woman in John 4:

"[Jesus] told her, "Go, call your husband and come back."

"I have no husband," she replied.

Jesus said to her, "You are right when you say you have no husband. The fact is, you have had five husbands, and the man you now have is not your husband. What you have just said is quite true."

"Sir," the woman said, "I can see that you are a prophet."

(vv. 16-19)

Jesus gave this lady one very specific piece of information about her life – she has had five husbands and was living with a man who was not her husband. That's it. One piece of insight into her secret history. And yet, that one piece of information opened her up to a deeper conversation which eventually led to spiritual harvest in her community.

We will deal with prophetic evangelism more in a later chapter, but for now, I want you to see how a simple word of knowledge unlocked the heart of someone who was desperately searching for satisfaction and fulfillment in all the wrong places.

People are longing to feel that they are seen and known. That they matter. That their life has some meaning and significance. A word of knowledge is a powerful, yet simple way of opening them up to the reality that there is a God in Heaven who loves them deeply and wants to be involved in their lives. The goal is not to amaze people with your prophetic accuracy but to connect them with the heart of the Father.

Also, this example from John 4 shows that a word of knowledge is often information about something in your past that God uses in some way to speak into your present.

What God reveals might be positive, or it may relate to strongholds or blockages in our lives caused by past events.

On the positive side, you may have a word about an individual having a legacy of compassion in their family. From there you could pray that God enlarges their own heart to carry on what He has deposited into their ancestors. Or perhaps, you may receive a word of knowledge that someone used to love writing but have put it aside. As you are praying with them, you may declare that God wants to unlock their creativity again and that they have a story to tell that needs to be expressed in a book.

Alternatively, you may receive a word that there has been occult involvement in someone's family history which is manifesting in some negative spiritual way today. As you pray into it, you will often see release and healing come into their life.

For many years I struggled with asthma. I couldn't run for more than 20 seconds without having to use an inhaler. Around 15 years ago, at a conference, I was asked by a leader if any of my family had ever been in a specific organization that exists here in Ireland. I responded that I am the only male in my family, through every generation, who has not been a member of that organization. A team prayed with me and I renounced any connection with that group. Two days later, I ran five kilometers. Soon I was running up to 40K a week. The word of knowledge had identified a spiritual blockage in my life which was preventing experiencing physical health and wholeness. It can be an incredibly valuable tool as we counsel and minister to others.

USE IT TO GROW IT

I'm sure many of you have witnessed prophets, online or in-person, give highly specific words of knowledge to individuals in crowded auditoriums. They know names, addresses, the names of their kids and even their pets. While I enjoy watching clips like these on YouTube, I also find them a little frustrating and discouraging. The prophetic person seems so uniquely gifted and powerfully anointed that I'm not sure I could ever come close to what they are doing, so why bother even trying?

That's one of the main reasons why I've written this book. I like to think that I am very normal. There were no supernatural events surrounding my birth. I wasn't raised in a Christian home. I didn't see angels as a kid. I don't experience visions and trances on a regular basis. Nor have I ever heard the audible voice of God. I'm just a Christ-follower who believes that God longs to speak to His children and I am learning to grow in my ability to hear him. And I am absolutely convinced that you can hear Him too.

Honestly, if you had told me just a few years ago that I would be sharing words of knowledge about stranger's names, birthdays and wedding anniversaries, I would have really struggled to believe it. However, like any skill, as we step out in faith and use whatever measure of ability we currently have in hearing God's voice, it will grow and develop over time. You must be willing to risk and fail.

There is just no other way. But, if you earnestly desire to hear Him with more frequency and clarity, I promise, it will come.

Finally, I only ever share my secrets with friends who I am sure I can trust. God is the same. When it comes to the prophetic, we long for accuracy, but God is looking for intimacy. Everything flows out of relationship with Him. He doesn't want us simply to know what He knows but to feel what He feels and to see people how He sees them. Once we really understand this, we will not only communicate knowledge that informs but supernatural revelation that transforms. It's not about impressing people but expressing the heart of the Father.

In the next chapter, we'll explore giving and receiving words of knowledge in greater detail.

Practical Exercise: The next time you are praying for someone, ask God to give you one specific piece of information or insight about them that you don't already know. It could be a name, a date, an event that took place, some particular food they like, etc. Don't limit it to any category. Then, simply ask them about it. You could be wrong. But you could also be amazed that you are right. The only way to grow is to practice, so please take risks and make mistakes.

DAY 15

HOW GOD SPEAKS: WORDS OF KNOWLEDGE // PART 2

"Prophecy is different from the Word of Knowledge in that Prophecy has to do with conveying a message from the voice of Christ whereas the Word of Knowledge has to do with expressing part of the mind of Christ... The Word of Knowledge tends to deal more with information regarding the past and present. Rather than expressing a message, it tends to have more to do with facts surrounding events, thoughts, intentions, actions, ideas, and other such things."

(Art Thomas)

I was growing increasingly frustrated with God. In fact, I would say that deep disappointment was beginning to settle into my heart.

I had been an Assistant Pastor for just over four years. In my particular denomination, it's normal to spend a maximum of three years as an Assistant before you move on to leading a church as Senior Pastor. Yet, no opportunities were being presented to me. I had just been to a pastor's conference where, upon hearing how long I had been an Assistant, one of the attendees had blurted out,

"Wow, what have you done wrong!" At that moment, I had wanted to give him the 'right hand of fellowship' to the side of his head!

But he was only expressing how I felt deep down. Perhaps I had done something wrong. Maybe the Lord was angry with me. Or, could it be, as I had prayed numerous times, "God, have you forgotten about me?"

In the midst of my internal struggles, I had a rare Sunday free from ministry. I decided to attend another church around 30 minutes from where I lived. I don't remember anything about the service that day, except that I had been battling a really bad sinus infection. I felt lousy, physically and emotionally. At the end of the message, the pastor called forward anyone who needed prayer for healing. I felt so rotten that I reluctantly made my way to the front.

I informed the young man on the prayer team that I wanted prayer for my sinus condition. He began to pray for healing. Then he stopped. Tentatively he said, "I don't know who you are or what you do, but I believe the Lord wants to say something to you and it's about your job. He simply wants to tell you that He hasn't forgotten about you."

Tears trickled down my cheeks. It was such a short and simple word, almost generic. Yet, it was precisely what I needed to hear at that moment.

Within three months, two different churches came knocking on my door. One of them, a struggling congregation in inner-city Dublin, was where we spent the next five years, seeing God do the most incredible things. God hadn't forgotten about me.

SNIPPETS FROM THE MIND OF CHRIST

In an earlier chapter, we saw how Jesus told the disciples that the Holy Spirit "will receive from me what he will make known to you." (John 16: 15)

There is nothing that Jesus doesn't know. There is no subject in which He is not an expert. There are no secrets hidden from Him. Colossians 2:3 tells us that "....in him are hidden all the treasures of wisdom and knowledge." The Word of Knowledge is simply when the Holy Spirit takes from Christ's omniscient knowledge and makes it known to you. It is a glimpse into the mind of Christ by which we share in His 'knowing' about a specific thought, incident, or intention.

Very often a Word of Knowledge will come as a simple thought that pops into your mind. It will seem random, because, in a sense, it is. Random to you, but not to the Holy Spirit.

For example, you might be praying for someone and, out of nowhere, think about a country that you know nothing about. This happened to me a few years ago. In our small group, I was praying with a young entrepreneur. Out of the blue, I found myself thinking about Indonesia, Brazil, and South Africa. They were just three unconnected countries that somehow entered my mind. If you were to give me a map, the only one I could point out is South Africa. Therefore, I knew these couldn't be my natural thoughts. I shared them and, sure enough, the businessman confirmed that these were the very three countries that they were looking at expanding into.

I once heard Mike Pilavachi, who leads Soul Survivor in the UK, recount a story about something that happened when he was a guest speaker in a church. He was half-way through his message when lyrics from a completely random song came into his mind: "Won't you come home Bill Bailey, won't you come home?"

He tried to ignore the distraction and continue preaching. Yet, he couldn't shake the words of this old Bobby Darin song. Eventually, he stopped his message and said: "I know this probably sounds ridiculous, but I keep hearing the words: 'Won't you come home Bill Bailey, won't you come home?'"

A man seated in the back row of the church immediately started sobbing loudly. After the meeting, he shared his story.

His name wasn't Bill Bailey, it was Jack Bailey. Two weeks before this, after a heated argument with his wife, he had stormed out of the house, also leaving behind his two young children. Too stubborn to go home, he had been living in cheap hotels and shelters. On that particular evening, he was walking the streets, cold and wet. He passed the church, and upon seeing the doors open, decided to go in simply to get some warmth. Within ten minutes of entering the building, he hears the words: "Won't you come home Bill Bailey, won't you come home?"

The church leadership prayed with him, drove him home, and he was reconciled with his family.

We have all had those sorts of random thoughts at different times. Most often we ignore them, putting them down to our own imagination or inability to concentrate. They seem like a distraction from the task at hand. Yet, if we were to pause and give them some attention, we might discover that the Holy Spirit is sharing with us some small snippet of Jesus' vast knowledge about a person or situation.

We need to grasp that God cares so deeply about every aspect of our lives, no matter how small or seemingly insignificant. As Bill Johnson says: "If it matters to you, it matters to Him." He wants to help us navigate through both the ordinary and the unusual circumstances of life. He longs to speak through you to give other people comfort, direction, encouragement, and correction. Words of Knowledge are a simple, yet powerful, way by which He says:

"I see you, I know you, I care about you." They realign God's children into their truest identity, value, and purpose.

IT'S NOT ABOUT PERFORMANCE

Other types of revelatory gifts, such as prophecy and visions, take time to play out and often need to be interpreted and pondered. The Word of Knowledge, on the other hand, is an immediate and instantaneous revelation. It's rather black and white. If you ask, "Does the date July 15th mean anything to you?", you'll either receive a 'yes' or 'no' answer. If you ask someone if their name is Susan, and it's actually Jane, there's not much room to manoeuvre there! This makes this a high-risk gift. You can end up feeling silly and embarrassed.

The problem is, when we retreat from using this gift because of fear, we are placing the focus on ourselves. We are attaching it to our 'performance' and 'success rate'. From God's perspective, it is always about the other person. Therefore, we must let go of our ego and desire to look good. Remember, prophetic revelation is always about strengthening, encouraging, and comforting.

A number of years ago, I was preaching in one of the largest churches in Ireland, led by the national leader of the Assemblies of

God. It was my first time there and, honestly, I wanted to impress this man. During the first service, as I preached, my attention was continually drawn to a family sitting in the back row. The word I felt the Spirit give me was: "Tell them 'well done'. They have been faithful. It wasn't their fault." I tried to ignore the prompting, but it wouldn't go away. At the time, I didn't know if this particular church permitted the use of spiritual gifts in this way. Plus, I had a message to preach and my time was short. I allowed the pressure to perform to stop me from sharing the word God had given me.

After the service, I spoke to the Associate Pastor about what God had shown me about that particular family. His face lit up and he said, "No way! They have just returned this past week from the mission field. They left Ireland last year full of faith, but they encountered so much opposition and discouragement that they had no option but to return home. They really feel as if they have failed God."

I was so annoyed and angry with myself. But mostly, I felt sorry for this family. Can you imagine what this simple word of encouragement that God had given me would have meant to them? I had allowed my desire to impress man cause me to disobey the Lord. I repented that day and told the Father I would never allow that to happen again.

If you give a word and it's wrong, that's okay. Own up to it. Please don't try to manipulate it or force it by saying something like: "Well, do you know someone called Susan?" Most people know someone by that name. People see through that stuff and it gives the prophetic ministry a bad reputation. There is so much more integrity in simply saying, "Okay, I got that wrong. I'm still learning to hear God's voice."

Also, don't assume that because you got part of a word wrong, that God has nothing else to share with that person through you. I know of situations where the initial detail shared was inaccurate, but the rest of the word was completely spot on.

Shawn Bolz says this:

"If I'm wrong with a word of knowledge, I can just move on, do some course correction, or even stop with that particular interaction. Being wrong doesn't disqualify or negate the accurate things I've said. It just means I'm still learning how to connect to and translate God."

Don't let your insecurities ruin a beautiful expression of the Father's love. Of course, there's risk. You will get it wrong. But when you get it right and speak God's mind and heart directly into someone's personal situation, the sense of joy and fulfillment you experience makes the risk so worthwhile.

Never forget, your identity comes through Christ, not through your performance in spiritual gifts. You are not under pressure to be 'right'. You are under covenant as a son or daughter who is unconditionally loved. Your goal is not to be accurate, but to express the Father's heart.

GROWING IN WORDS OF KNOWLEDGE

As you grow in sharing Words of Knowledge, you will start to instinctively sense what is 'from God' and what is 'from you'. When it's from God, as you begin to share the word, you will feel a different 'weight' upon it. It carries a different measure of authority. It's hard to describe, but you'll just know. You will also learn when to stop talking because you are in danger of moving from 'spirit' to 'flesh'. A gentle flow and ease will come as you 'get out of your own head' and focus on the Lord and the other person.

Over time, as you continue to develop in this gift, you may receive more than just basic information about people. God could begin to impart strategic wisdom, counsel, and insight for people, organizations and even governmental bodies.

I once heard Julian Adams, a respected prophet from South Africa, share how the CEO of one of the largest financial companies in Singapore brought him in to meet individually with their top tier management. He knew absolutely nothing about their industry. Yet, as he sat across the desk from each executive, God began to download clear and specific strategies and insights related to their roles. More than that though, he began to directly speak into their personal lives and situations. Understandably, God deeply impacted these men and women who, by all external appearances, had everything. The business insights were helpful. Yet, what they needed most was to know that there was a God in Heaven who loved them deeply.

God doesn't want to give us information or even revelation. He wants to give us Himself. In Him is all knowledge, wisdom and understanding. Like the vine and branches illustration taught by Jesus (John 15), He wants you to be so intimately and intricately connected to Him that all He is, and all He has, flows to and through you and begins to touch the world around you.

Practical Exercise: Get a pen and paper. Go onto a social media platform such as Facebook or Instagram. Select a friend/follower who you know, but aren't intimately acquainted with (preferably a believer).

Simply sit with their profile in front of you and ask God if there is anything that He wants you to share with them.

Jot down any random thoughts, images, words, or other information.

Pray over what you have written but don't overthink it.

If you sense that some of it could be relevant/pertinent, share it with them.

Simply drop them a message and say something like: "Hi ___, I was on Facebook today and when I saw your profile I randomly thought about new shoes. I know, weird, right?! Can I ask, are you stepping into any new role or position in the next while?"

Imagine a possible reply: "Yes! I'm actually starting a new job next week."

"That's so good. God wants you to know that He is with you and is directing your steps. I'll be praying for you."

Another possible reply: "No, I'm pretty settled where I am."

"Okay, well I think God wants you to know He's directing your steps. He loves you so much. Be blessed!"

DAY 16

HOW GOD SPEAKS: DISCERNMENT // PART 1

"God loves to speak to us to help us navigate life with victory as we discern both His plans and the plans of darkness. His voice directs, comforts and empowers us and provides every necessary insight for us to accomplish our divine assignments, to confront dark powers and to live lives that are pleasing to Him."

(Jane Hamon)

I was standing at a bus stop in Dublin when a young man walked past. At that moment, I sensed intense malevolence and evil emanating from this, otherwise, normal-looking twenty-something. The demonic presence took me by surprise. I looked around and noticed that he was now standing around two meters away from me, presumably waiting for the same bus. Under my breath, I began to pray in tongues. The young man became noticeably uncomfortable. I continued to pray. He grew increasingly anxious, now looking around him at each of the other people waiting at the stop. I kept praying in the Spirit, the man becoming very agitated and restless. Then he ran! Literally, he sprinted across the busy road, narrowly avoiding traffic and ran up the street, occasionally looking behind him as if someone or something was following him.

Have you ever been in a situation like this? Perhaps not as extreme. But where someone or something looked normal, but you just sense something is 'off'? Perhaps you walk into a meeting, even in church, and while people are worshipping and there's nothing unusual or abnormal happening, you just have an uneasy feeling. It can be very difficult to describe or define. It's almost like when you open your fridge and immediately subtly smell that something in there has passed its expiration date.

It can range from a simple 'gut' reaction to an internal sense of deep distress. You have a foreboding feeling of darkness and danger.

The discerning of spirits is one of the least discussed ways that God speaks to us. Paul lists this as one of the nine manifestations of the Holy Spirit in 1 Corinthians 12: 8-10:

"To one there is given through the Spirit…distinguishing between spirits…"

Other translations say "discerning of spirits" (ESV) and "the ability to discern whether a message is from the Spirit of God or from another spirit" (NLT).

The word translated 'discerning' in Greek is *diakriseis*, a combination of two words *dia*, meaning 'through' and *krisis* meaning 'judgment'. The gift of discernment, therefore, is the ability to judge, evaluate and perceive something in the spiritual realm.

Paul uses the word *pneuma* for spirits here. It is commonly used in three ways in the New Testament. The first refers to the 'spirit' within human beings. It is used in both a spiritual and psychological sense. For example, Luke in Acts 18:25 says that Apollos was "burning in spirit", indicating he had an intense spiritual fervor. Paul, elsewhere in Corinthians, uses the term "a spirit of meekness" (1 Cor 4: 21), clearly denoting an emotional or mental disposition. Sometimes, when presented with an issue, it's very difficult to discern what is spiritual and what is mental or emotional. We are complex beings and the two are often intertwined.

The second main use of this word is in connection with the Spirit of God. When Paul says, "God revealed it to us by his Spirit" (1 Cor 2: 10), he uses the word *pneuma*. In fact, when talking about the gifts of the Spirit in 1 Corinthians 12, he uses the same Greek word.

The third main usage refers to supernatural beings. These 'spirits' can be either good or evil. In Hebrews 1: 14, we read

"Are not all angels ministering spirits sent to serve those who will inherit salvation?"

The writer uses the word 'pneuma' in relation to angels. Angels are spirit beings that serve God and His people.

The same word pneuma is also used to describe demons in Mark 1: 23-26

"Just then a man in their synagogue who was possessed by an impure spirit (*pneuma*) cried out, "What do you want with us, Jesus of Nazareth? Have you come to destroy us? I know who you are - the Holy One of God!"

"Be quiet!" said Jesus sternly. "Come out of him!" The impure spirit (*pneuma*) shook the man violently and came out of him with a shriek."

To summarize, the word spirit, *pneuma*, can refer to the human spirit, the Holy Spirit, to unholy (demonic) spirits, and to angelic spirits. So, when Paul writes about 'discerning of spirits', he is referring to the ability to judge which of the above spirits are behind a particular action, event, behavior, or phenomenon.

DISCERNING THE HUMAN SPIRIT

When Jesus encountered Nathaniel in John 1, he discerned his human spirit, declaring that Nathaniel was "a man in whom there was no deceit." (v. 47) He had a 'guileless spirit'. When we talk about the human spirit, we may perceive or discern that someone has an anxious spirit, a proud spirit, a rebellious spirit, a heavy spirit, a jealous spirit, an angry spirit, a bitter spirit, a lustful spirit, a kind spirit, etc. Again, of course, there may be other spirits connected to these, but primarily it is related to the condition of the individual's heart and emotions.

When a group of people comes together, such as in a church gathering, you will often pick up on the predominant spirit in the room. You will 'feel' it in the atmosphere. Sometimes, in worship, I feel a heaviness in the room. I, therefore, know that many people are carrying burdens or worries so I might pray specifically into that. Or there could be an unusual sense of joy or celebration in the room. In that case, we press in for more.

DISCERNING THE HOLY SPIRIT

Next, we come to discerning the work of the Holy Spirit. Over the years, I have been in many gatherings with all sorts of weird and bizarre phenomena. As I have watched people roll on the ground, laugh hysterically, and even bark like dogs, I have sought to discern if this was truly the Holy Spirit at work. In some cases, I believe it was. In others, it was a mixture of God's Spirit, human emotion and psycho-suggestion, and even demonic manifestations.

Paul exhorts the church to distinguish between spirits in the context of prophetic utterances. In 1 Corinthians 14: 29 he writes:

"Two or three prophets should speak, and the others should weigh carefully what is said."

Once again, the original Greek for 'weigh carefully' is the word *diakrisis*, the same word he uses when describing the gift of discernment. In other words, when we encounter spiritual manifestations, even in a Christian setting, we shouldn't always automatically assume that what we are witnessing is the work of the Holy Spirit.

Of course, we don't want to become heresy hunters or spiritual 'sniffer dogs' constantly on the lookout for error. But when something feels 'off' in your spirit, you shouldn't ignore what you are sensing. In 1 John 4: 1, we are exhorted by the Apostle John:

"Beloved, do not believe every spirit, but **test the spirits** to see whether they are from God, for many false prophets have gone out."

Unfortunately, not everything that calls itself Christian or even sounds Christian, is Christian. Sometimes it is obvious that something is not of God, other times we need to step back and ask the Lord if this is truly His work. The Holy Spirit wants to help us discern the spiritual source of what we are seeing or hearing.

DISCERNING DEMONIC SPIRITS

On one occasion, a young lady who had apparently just returned from missions in Africa asked to meet with me. As soon as I opened the door of the church to let her in, my spiritual antennae went into overdrive. She looked perfectly normal, but there was an intense demonic presence emanating from her. I told my assistant to stay close by during the meeting.

Throughout the conversation, she came across as hyper-spiritual. I always find it uncomfortable when anyone uses too much 'Christianese'. Often it signifies that the person is attempting to cover up deeper issues. As the meeting progressed, the young lady described bizarre different spiritual experiences she had while in Africa. She found them exhilarating, I found them downright weird. Honestly, I wanted to conclude my time with her as quickly as possible, so I suggested that I pray with her. She agreed, as long as I would lay hands on her, as she longed for a 'spiritual impartation'. Inside me, the Holy Spirit was shouting: "Do not touch her!"

I told her that I would pray, but not by the laying on of hands. (On a side note, Paul warns us: "Do not lay hands on anyone hastily…" (1 Tim 5: 22)) She told me that she really wanted an impartation and that she would prefer if I placed my hands on her. Once again I said that I was happy to pray, but I would not lay hands on her. Not satisfied with that outcome, she got up to leave.

I walked behind her down the stairs, wanting to ensure that she exited the building. Halfway down, she attempted to corner me, once again demanding that I lay hands on her. Much more sternly now, I looked her in the eyes and declared, "I will not lay hands on you. In the name of Jesus, I command you to leave right now." For a moment, her face contorted with rage. I repeated, (In Jesus' name, get out now!" Her body jerked, and she walked with haste towards the door.

A few weeks later, before a Sunday service, I happened to walk through one of the kid's ministry rooms. The lights weren't on and it was dark inside. Again, I sensed an evil presence. I turned around at the door and there was the same young woman crouched down in the corner. I'm not sure exactly what she was doing, but I knew it wasn't good. I told her to leave the room immediately. She stayed around the back of the main church auditorium until the service began, but as soon as we started to worship, she immediately exited the building and never returned.

Jesus often discerned demonic spirits at work beneath the surface of a person's life. We see the same in Acts 13 with Peter and the magician Elymas and in Acts 16 with Paul and the psychic slave girl.

It goes without saying, that in our culture today, there has been a significant increase in recent years in occultism, paganism, mysticism, and satanism. Therefore, the importance of discerning spirits cannot be overestimated. We need to know if demonic spirits are at work in individuals, organizations, systems, and communities.

DISCERNING ANGELIC SPIRITS

Later in this book, we will explore the angelic realm in greater detail as this is one of the primary ways God communicates with His people throughout Scripture.

Perhaps one of the most familiar examples in the Bible is when the prophet Elisha finds himself surrounded in a city by the army of the King of Syria. Elisha reassures his servant not to be afraid because those who were with them outnumbered those who were against them. From a physical, visible perspective, this wasn't true. They were completely overpowered. However, when Elisha prayed, "Open his eyes, LORD, so that he may see" (2 Kings 6: 17), the servant became aware of the invisible, angelic realm all around them.

So, discernment can sometimes reveal the presence of angels. I have found this to be most often true in worship gatherings. I will sense the presence of angels in a certain part of the room. My wife occasionally sees two angels standing behind me as I preach. I am deeply thankful for these ministering spirits sent to serve those who belong to Christ (Hebrews 1: 14)

IS IT ME OR GOD?

As with all prophetic revelation, we must seek to determine if what we are sensing is genuinely coming from the Holy Spirit, or is it simply our personal feelings being filtered through our past experiences. For example, if we hear a preacher and 'discern' something 'off', could it be due to our previous negative church encounters with people in positions of authority? Maybe he or she even reminds us of someone from our past. Ephesians 1: 17 speaks of having a spirit of "wisdom and revelation". We need both, otherwise our own opinions and prejudices can block us from seeing what is happening in the natural and spiritual realms. Having mature believers and leaders around us can keep us from falling into the trap of 'serial suspicion', where we become overly judgemental and critical of anyone who doesn't conform to what we consider to be 'sound'.

The other danger is that we become so overwhelmed with what we are discerning and sensing in the spiritual realm that we shut down the gift. We become frustrated with our own inability to know what to do with the revelations we are receiving, or we make mistakes and unintentionally hurt other people.

In the next chapter, we will further explore this much-needed gift of discernment, looking at how we steward it with wisdom, and also how we discern the times we are living in so that we can walk with vision and victory. As Jane Hamon says, "Spiritual discernment gives us a strategic advantage to win every battle."

Practical Exercise: Over the next few days, when you walk into any room or environment, pause for a few moments and ask the Lord to show you what is happening spiritually in that place. Look around, take everything in, see beyond the surface. What do you sense in your spirit? Practice becoming more aware of what is happening in the invisible realm all around you, all the time.

DAY 17

HOW GOD SPEAKS: DISCERNMENT // PART 2

"The number one weapon the devil deploys in the last days isn't the mark of the beast, radical Islam, or a nuclear holocaust. His number one weapon is deception. The chief description of Satan's activity in the book of Revelation is that he is "the deceiver of the whole world" whose primary activity is accomplished as he "goes forth to deceive the nations." (See Revelation 12:9; 20:8.) If his number one weapon is deception, the number one gift most needed (and most frequently absent) in the body of Christ is the discerning of spirits!"

(Lance Wallnau)

A number of years ago, I led a church where the founding pastor had fallen into immorality. This sad situation had happened around 10 years before I arrived. It turned out that he had covered up his sin for around two years before it was exposed and he was subsequently asked to leave. I asked various people who had been around at that time if they ever had any sense of what was going on. Many of them said the same thing: "We knew something was wrong. His messages sounded as good as they used to. But there was no power in them any longer. It was as if something had lifted off him."

On the surface, everything appeared the same. And yet, through human discernment and the Holy Spirit, people are able to 'pick up' that something had shifted and that the anointing was gone.

In the last chapter I made it clear that as we think about discernment, we don't want to become overly negative, focusing on "demon hunting" and sniffing out evil spirits. However, we are living at a time when there has never been a greater need for discernment within the Body of Christ. Many believers seem to be incredibly naïve and readily accept any unusual spiritual manifestation as being from God. Increasingly, we are a very experience-oriented generation who build our lives and make decisions based on feelings rather than on the Word of God. If it feels good it must be good, right? Therefore, deception is rife within and outside the church. And the enemy has a field day, as lives are destroyed, marriages fall apart, and churches are damaged and divided.

James Goll is right when he says:
"The unseen supernatural reality around us is populated with both angels and demons, and human beings are notoriously poor at

telling the difference between good spirits and bad ones."

What makes it even more difficult is that there can be a mixture of the Spirit and the flesh operating in the same environment. Like the parable of the wheat and the weeds that Jesus told in Matthew 13, both good and evil may manifest together in the same season. Anything the Holy Spirit does, the enemy will try to subvert and spoil.

A number of years ago there were extended revival meetings in Lakeland, Florida. Many Christian leaders I spoke to had serious misgivings about these. While I definitely sensed that there was something "off" with aspects of what I witnessed, I also believed that God's Spirit was genuinely at work there. In fact, I attended some local meetings connected with this move and was powerfully impacted by the Lord.

After some time, it came to light that the leader of the revival had started having an affair with someone involved in the meetings. He left his wife and the whole thing fell apart abruptly. While all of this is heartbreaking, it shows how easily the enemy can infiltrate something (and someone) that I believe could have been used powerfully by the Spirit.

TEST THE SPIRITS

While none of us ever want to quench the genuine work of the Holy Spirit, the Bible does make it very clear that we are to test the spirits:

"Do not despise prophecies. Test all things; hold fast what is good."
(1 Thessalonians 5:20–21)

The Bible also teaches that we are to train ourselves to discern good from evil so we can become mature as believers (Heb 5: 14). Therefore, we should not feel guilty for questioning or taking time to evaluate a particular movement or ministry, as long as we are doing it with a heart of love and honor.

So how can we discern if it's the Holy Spirit, the human spirit, a demonic spirit, or an angelic spirit at work? There are some questions we can ask which will help us along the way.

CRITERIA FOR DISCERNMENT

The Test of Conviction
We need to remember that, though we all have some natural ability to discern good from evil, ultimately it is a gift given by the Holy

Spirit. While there is some element of intuition involved, it is much more than that. Those who have this gift don't just sense something is 'off' about a person or situation. They feel it deeply. This could manifest physically and emotionally as nausea, feeling 'dirty', unsettledness, lack of peace, agitation, righteous anger, even anxiety. It can't be shaken or ignored.

When Paul was being pursued by the clairvoyant slave girl in Acts 16, we are told that he eventually became "greatly troubled". This was no gentle irritation. It was a discernment of an unclean spirit because we read in verse 18:
"Finally Paul became so annoyed that he turned around and said to the spirit, "In the name of Jesus Christ I command you to come out of her!" At that moment the spirit left her."

At a worship gathering in Ireland, one evening two males performed what was supposed to be a 'prophetic dance'. Honestly, to me, it fell somewhere between immoral and just plain weird. I was so overwhelmed with disgust that I had to get out of the meeting. I literally couldn't sit through it. Another leader from our church was sitting in a different part of the church with his family. He had the exact same reaction. I met him in the hallway as we hastily exited!

The Test of Community

The most common use of the gift of discernment, according to Paul, was in a public worship gathering. He insisted that spiritual manifestations should be weighed and evaluated by the others in attendance, not only the leaders. Discernment, therefore, is a communal responsibility. Together we make a judgment.

I once attended Sunday worship service at a church in Los Angeles. As we entered into an extended time of worship, something just didn't feel right. It seemed as if the band were more concerned with performing than worshipping. All of the songs were about 'me' rather than about 'Him'. I tried to close my eyes and ignore what I was feeling, as I really wanted to engage with the Lord. Plus, I didn't want to be critical or negative. But, honestly, it was as if the Spirit had left the building. Eventually, I opened my eyes and sat down. As I looked around, I saw that probably one half of the congregation was also seated and disengaged. It was as if the faith community had together discerned the absence of God's presence and that there was another spirit at work.

We all have our own biases and prejudices based on our personal history and experiences and therefore it can be so helpful to have insight from others when we are seeking to make spiritual evaluations about people, places, and movements. We don't want to write something off simply because it's not to our taste. Nor do we want to wholeheartedly embrace someone's ministry because they exhibit spiritual power that we find attractive. All of the parts of the body have an important role to play.

The Test of Consistency

This involves asking if the particular phenomenon is consistent with (i) the Spirit of Jesus; (ii) the Scriptures; (iii) the way God has clearly worked in the past.

When I talk about the 'Spirit of Jesus', it's simply asking: does this sound and look like Jesus? Is it consistent with the nature and character of Christ as revealed in God's Word? If anyone speaks or acts in a way completely contrary to how Jesus would, we should seriously question their motives or ministry.

It should also go without saying that nothing should be permitted which is prohibited by or contrary to Scripture, however powerful or plausible it may feel.

Likewise, if something has absolutely no legitimate precedent in church history it should be treated with caution.

Of course, God often does a 'new thing' and we want to be open to that. But what is 'new' to us will likely have been part of the experience of believers at some stage during the last 2000 years.

The Test of Christ-Centredness

This is simply asking: does this glorify Christ? Is this pointing to the finished work of Jesus? Is it exalting the eternal Son of God who became a man and is now seated at the right hand of the Father?

This was clearly a big issue in the early church, which is why the Apostle John wrote:

"Dear friends, do not believe every spirit, but test the spirits to see whether they are from God, because many false prophets have gone out into the world. This is how you can recognize the Spirit of God: Every spirit that acknowledges that Jesus Christ has come in the flesh is from God, but every spirit that does not acknowledge Jesus is not from God. This is the spirit of the antichrist, which you have heard is coming and even now is already in the world."
(1 John 4:1–3)

The Holy Spirit primarily reveals and glorifies Jesus. Therefore any spiritual experience which does not draw people's hearts towards the Lord Jesus Christ should be treated with suspicion.

The Test of Character

The gifts of the Spirit can never be divorced from the fruit of the Spirit (Gal 5: 20-22). Sadly, the history of Christianity is littered with incredibly anointed men and women who came to ruin and brought the church into disrepute because their gifting exceeded their character.

No one is perfect and we should never write anybody off because of a past failure or indiscretion. However, when there is a repeated pattern of ungodly living and unrepentant sin, we should not endorse or support that ministry or individual.

The Test of Consequence

We have already seen that true prophecy results in God's people being strengthened, encouraged and comforted. The church is built up and grows up. The saints are equipped, exhorted, and edified. In other words, good prophecy brings good fruit. Jesus himself said that we would recognize prophets by their fruit (Matthew 7: 20). Therefore, if any ministry leads to pride, dishonesty, immorality or greed, it is clearly not honoring the Holy Spirit.

This is true of all spiritual phenomena, not just prophecy. If it is truly motivated by the Holy Spirit, then the fruit of it will be good. We, therefore, need to recognize that this will at times require a delay in making a judgment. Fruit doesn't grow overnight. It may take time to see what is produced by a ministry or manifestation. Take prophecy for example. It could take months or even years before you see a prophetic word come to pass. Having said that, if someone has a track record of being completely inaccurate, you can probably safely assume that they're not operating under the anointing of God's Spirit.

I always try to err on the side of grace. However, we cannot afford to be naïve or gullible. We have a real enemy who wants to steal, kill, and destroy the work of God in our lives and in our churches (John 10: 10). False prophets are real and don't typically dress like wolves. Unclean spirits can gain footholds in some of the most gifted people and appealing places. Satan himself masquerades as an angel of light (2Cor 11: 14).

In brief, here is a good checklist to use when we are attempting to discern the source of a spiritual phenomenon:

1. Is it your gut reaction that this is of the Lord?
2. Are others witnessing that this is the Holy Spirit?
3. Is it consistent with the character of Jesus, as revealed in Scripture?
4. Is it consistent with the Word of God and with orthodox Christian doctrine?

5. Does this draw attention to the Lord Jesus Christ or to someone or something else?
6. Is it frenzied, uncontrolled, and disorderly?
7. Is it expressed in a loving manner?
8. What kind of fruit do you think this will produce?

Ultimately, we need to depend fully on the Holy Spirit to teach and train us to discern truth from error. As James Goll says:

"We must value the anointing of the Holy Spirit because He helps us apply every test. We cannot take the anointing of the Spirit for granted, even if we have years and years of experience of walking with God. Besides the general anointing we receive when the Holy Spirit comes to live within us, by which Jesus said we are guided into all truth (John 16:13)."

Practical Exercise: Here is a prayer of activation from Jane Hamon, asking the Lord to increase within you the gift of discernment. Find a quiet spot at some stage today and pray this over your life:

Lord, I cry out for a deeper level of discernment than ever before. Give me eyes to see and ears to hear in the spirit realm. Sharpen my ability to hear Your voice and to be a watchman on the wall for my family, church, city and nation. Make me as one of the sons of Issachar. Help me to discern the times and strategies, to discern demons and demonic structures. Let me recognize the presence and operation of angels and angel armies and know how to work with them. Help me to be wise as I discern human spirits, and guard my heart from becoming judgmental or critical and from carrying false responsibility. Help me discern Your reformation plans and purposes so I can join the work of Your ekklesia in the earth, bringing Kingdom transformation and life everywhere I go. Anoint me to lead, to build and to war. Give me wisdom as I engage in spiritual battle, recognizing first and foremost that Jesus Christ already defeated every principality and power. Show me my part in the Kingdom so that I can accomplish every spiritual assignment You give me. Your people are on earth to enforce Your victory, extend and expand Your Kingdom and reveal Your glory. Lord, give me a discerning heart so I can stand among those called to "turn the world upside down." In the mighty name of Jesus Christ I pray, Amen!

DAY 18

HOW GOD SPEAKS: DISCERNMENT // PART 3

"Each of us needs to become a discerner - no matter what our personal background or specific gift or function in the body of Christ. Although some believers are especially gifted as prophets, every follower of Jesus receives the gifts of revelation and discernment. And every believer needs to use them! In fact, without discernment and sensitivity to the Holy Spirit, we cannot progress in our use of any of the gifts and callings."

(James Goll)

When we talk about discernment, we often think of the discerning of spirits. However, the Bible also talks about discerning the times and seasons we are living in. For example, we read in Daniel 2: 21:

"He changes times and seasons; he deposes kings and raises up others. He gives wisdom to the wise and knowledge to the discerning."

Daniel connects the changing of seasons with God giving His people wisdom and discernment.

As I write this chapter, it is mid-September. Here in Ireland, we are experiencing unusually warm weather for this time of year. Just a few days ago it was sunny and in the high 70's (24 degrees celsius). However, the previous week it was rainy and in the mid-40's! That's quite a difference in the matter of a few days. Summer is doing all it can to stay around, while autumn is determined to press in. It feels as if we're stuck between seasons. It's difficult to know what clothes to wear or to make plans for activities. Each morning I check the forecast and look outside before I start to get ready.

It can be even more difficult to determine what season you are entering in other areas of your life. Especially in a year like 2020, where everything has been so significantly disrupted and disorientating. What is God doing – in the wider world and in my life? Those are very important questions to ask right now.

DISCERNING THE TIMES

Jesus said this to the Pharisees and Sadducees who were trying to test Him:

"When it is evening you say, 'It will be fair weather, for the sky is red'; and in the morning, 'It will be foul weather today, for the sky is red and threatening.' Hypocrites! You know how to discern the face of the sky, but you cannot discern the signs of the times." (Matthew 16:2–3)

Jesus was rebuking the religious leaders of his day, urging them not to judge matters merely by what they viewed with their natural eyes but rather to see with the eyes of the spirit and respond accordingly. Here was the promised Messiah, the One about whom the prophets had written so much, standing right before them. Yet, because He didn't fit into their religious expectations, they failed to perceive the day of His visitation (Luke 19: 41-44).

As prophetic people, we must seek to understand God's times and seasons and align ourselves to them properly or we will miss the fullness of what God is doing.

God is often doing a completely new thing while His people are still camped around the last thing He did. Or we're stuck in an old mindset which reflects the way we think He 'should' do things. That's why we are urged to "keep in step with the Spirit" (Gal 5: 25). We have a tendency to lag behind and can be slow to catch up with the activity of God in us and around us. However, if we ask, I believe that God will give us eyes to see and ears to hear so that we can properly discern the times and position ourselves with His purposes.

WHAT TIME IS IT?

In the New Testament, there are four different Greek words for time, each having a specific meaning:

Aion means "an age, eternity, everlasting, always." It refers to the eternal nature and rule of God.

Chronos refers to what we call 'chronological' time, which is the normal passing of time in hours, days, weeks and years. It can also be translated 'seasons' as the four seasons are part of our chronological calendar. From the moment we are conceived until we go to be with the Lord, our whole lives take place in *chronos*.

Kairos means "a set time, an opportune time, a due season, a moment of intervention". Acts 17: 26 says that God has determined the "appointed times (*kairos*) in history". A *kairos* moment can shift everything. Heaven and earth converge and there is an opportunity to be seized. A *kairos* interrupts *chronos*. God breaks in. There are favor, resources and breakthrough available, but only if we are able to discern the *kairos* moment.

Hora means "an hour, instant, definite time, point of time". *Hora* is similar to *kairos*. It is the 'now' time of God. In John 2, when pressed by his mother to do something about the lack of wine at the wedding in Cana, Jesus responded: "My hour (*hora*) has not yet come." (v. 4)

Hora takes the *kairos* season of God and brings it down to a specific, identifiable point when things change. At times Jesus would say something like: "The hour (hora) is coming and has now come...." (e.g. John 4: 23) He was saying, "Things have shifted. Change is here."

Putting all of this together, in the overarching, eternal plan of God (*aion*), there is the normal passing of time (*chronos*), which if responded to properly sets us up for the opportune times of favor and breakthrough (*kairos*). Within these kairos times are "now" moments (*hora*) for miracles. We must be sensitive to the Holy Spirit so we can shift our hearts and minds and align with our "now" seasons.

What about your own life right now?
You are going through your daily routines in *chronos* time. In the midst of that, do you perceive the Lord is doing something new? Is this a *kairos* or *horas* moment?
Have there been unusual happenings or divinely orchestrated 'coincidences'?

Are new doors opening or new desires growing?
Has there been abnormal spiritual warfare around your life?
Do you feel that a shift is imminent?
Or is there a sense of delay? As if something is being held up?

Take some time to think these through as you seek to discern the season you are in.

On a wider scale, as we look around the world, to the natural eye, things don't look particularly good. Yet, at this time of upheaval, I believe we are also in a season of *kairos*. Yes, there is so much darkness and even oppression all around us. Yet, I sense we are living in an Isaiah 60: 1-2 season:

"Arise, shine, for your light has come,
and the glory of the LORD rises upon you.
See, darkness covers the earth
and thick darkness is over the peoples,
but the LORD rises upon you
and his glory appears over you."

We are at a tipping point in many nations. Spiritual warfare is intense and seems to be increasing. At times, evil and injustice seem to be winning. But also, the church is being sifted and stirred. Many believers are waking up from their slumber of comfortable Christianity and realizing that we are in a battle. In the coming months, I believe that we will see the glory of the Lord break through the great darkness in many nations. The Lord will rise upon His people and display His power in unprecedented ways.

Chuck Pierce, in his book *The Best Is Yet Ahead*, gives us encouragement about how we can press toward our prophetic fulfillment:

"There are seasons in our lives that are now times - times of prophetic fulfillment when God's promises are manifested. In the natural cycle of life, there are seasons. Some seasons are filled with desolation: but in those times we can take comfort in knowing that every season has a time frame. There is a time when desolation ends and prophetic fulfillment begins. . . . Daniel knew it was time for the word to be fulfilled and captivity to end. We, like Daniel, also need to come to a place where we understand God's time sequence. In my own life I know that when it is time for a desolation season to end, I want it done and its effects off of me. And once I get out of it, I don't want to turn back. That's the attitude we need to have in moving forward into prophetic fulfillment. We need to be in close enough relationship to God so we know when to start into a new sequence and a new cycle of life. We need to know when it is time to cast off our desolation and move into a new season."

DON'T MISS YOUR MOMENT

In 1 Chronicles 12: 32 we read about the sons of Issachar. These were "men that had **understanding** of the times, to **know** what Israel ought to do."

The words *understand* and *know* are both the Hebrew word *yada*. Yada means "to know, to perceive, to discern, to distinguish, to discriminate, to be cunning, to advise, to have wit, to know by experience, to be skillful in, to be wise." This was not merely book knowledge but also personal understanding and prophetic revelation that were applied experientially. They had the power, as a unique breed of prophetic people in Israel, to see and know what was coming, and to discern strategies for how Israel was to position herself to receive a blessing.

If we are to navigate successfully through these turbulent and tumultuous times, we will need an 'Issachar anointing'. We must be able to discern what is going on behind the scenes spiritually so that we can respond effectively and strategically. This, I believe, is the Spirit of both "wisdom and revelation" that Paul talks about in Ephesians 1: 17. Revelation enables us to see what is happening and to hear God's voice; wisdom enables us to interpret it and respond properly in this new season.

It is vital that we not only know what season we are in but that we apply what we know and align our lives to receive all that God has for us. This may involve intercessory prayer, prophetic decrees and practical action. If we fail to act appropriately to what we discern the Lord saying, we can miss the benefit, blessing or opportunity that is available to us in that season.

In her book *Discernment*, Jane Hamon writes about how well-known prophet Cindy Jacobs once visited the area where she lived and prophesied that God was going to bring the local region into a time of prosperity and that real estate prices would skyrocket. Below is Jane Hamon's account of how she responded:

"Tom and I had lived in our area for fifteen years and real estate prices had gone up a bit but nothing to be described as skyrocketing. At the time of this prophetic word, we were struggling to make ends meet and were slow to respond. We had never done any investing of that sort, so we took a good deal of time investigating and learning about the market, and trying to figure out where the money would come from for us to invest. But others who had more knowledge and faith responded immediately by buying investment property. Within the year, many people experienced their land values exploding up to fifty times the amount they paid! Tom and I had prayed about the idea of a new season, made decrees accepting the new prosperity and investigated the topic, but we never put ourselves into a position to partake of it. This was one big experience to learn from!"

Whenever God speaks about a new season, we must be diligent to ask Him what we need to do to align with it. It takes discernment to see the new, but it also takes discernment to see the old we must let go of in order to embrace change.

We are living in what is probably the most significant and unusual time in modern history. To have any hope of navigating through this transition, we will have to lean into the Lord and seek His perspective on personal issues. Dutch Sheets words are very applicable to this season:

"Many of us have arrived at the place where we stand today only because we've been diligent to lean in to hear the voice of the Lord. Nonetheless, I feel very strongly in my spirit that to arrive at our next great horizon, we must go to a new level of listening, discerning and seeing in the Spirit. There is a new level of prophetic revelation God is inviting us to tap into that will take us to a greater level of authority and assignment.

There are new paradigms and strategies being released to the church that are vital for successfully moving forward into the next season. We cannot allow our attention to be divided. We must identify and remove anything that is crowding out His voice. Not only must we incline our ears to hear what Holy Spirit is saying to us, we must be willing to obey. We must bring ourselves under the authority of what we hear, to submit to it and follow it through to obedience."

Practical Exercise: In my book *The Tension of Transition*, I outline some signs of shifting seasons in our personal lives. Read the following excerpt and ask yourself if this your current experience. If so, take time aside with the Lord and ask Him how you need to practically respond *today* to this shift that is taking place.

HOW DO YOU RECOGNISE THAT YOU'RE SHIFTING SEASONS?

There are signs. Just as when you see the leaves turning orange and red you know its autumn, so there are also signs that you're transitioning or entering a new season.

Here are just a few of them:

- **Opposition or difficulty** can actually be a sign that you're entering a new season. It took a Goliath to move David from the shepherd boy season into the kingship season.

And sometimes that tension we feel is actually a sign of transition – we're moving from one season to another.

- **Closed doors** can be a sign of a new season. You're doing what used to get you results, but for some reason, it's not working anymore. No matter how much you try or how hard you push, you just seem to keep hitting a brick wall. It could be a sign that you're entering a new season.

- **Relational Shifts.** Some people who were central to your life either aren't there any longer or you just don't feel like you have the same connection anymore. And some new relationships have formed, maybe even with people who six months ago you would never have imagined having a connection with. It could be a sign that you are shifting seasons.

- **Changing Needs/Desires.** Things that used to bring you so much satisfaction and joy now don't really bring the same fulfillment. You're doing what you always do, but you're bored by it. You're getting the results you always wanted, and yet you feel flat and joyless. You spend each day thinking, "I can't keep doing this. Something has to change." It could be a sign that you are shifting seasons.

- **Feelings of Constriction.** You feel contained in a certain area of your life. It's like you have grown, but your environment around you has stayed the same, and now it feels really small, limiting, and almost suffocating. You know there's more inside you than what people are seeing, and you need to be stretched. It's almost like when the baby in the womb reaches nine months. It has to come out. It can't be contained anymore without harm being caused to both the mother and baby. That feeling of constriction can be a sign in your life that God is birthing a new season.

- **A New Joy or Sense of Freedom.** For the last, while you've felt discouraged and discontent – but you now find yourself passionate about life again. It's like the spark has come back, there's a freshness in your life. Doors that seemed closed have now started to open. There are opportunities and possibilities that there haven't been in a very long time. You are shifting into a new season.

Right now there is a significant shift in seasons taking place for some of you. It's unsettling, unnerving, but also very exciting. Enter into the fullness of all that the Father has prepared for you.

DAY 19

HOW PROPHECY COMES FORTH

"Although prophecy comes <u>through</u> the mouth or pen of people, it comes <u>from</u> the mind of God."

(James Goll)

Late in the afternoon on December 30th 2019, I pressed the 'RECORD' button on the voice dictation app on my phone. All that day I had been sensing something stirring and bubbling inside me. It's hard to describe, but it felt as if there was something inside me that I had to release. I have learned that this is one sign that the Holy Spirit *within* me is signaling that He wants to say something *through* me. It's similar to what Jeremiah expressed when he said: "…his word is in my heart like a fire, a fire shut up in my bones. I am weary of holding it in; indeed, I cannot." (Jeremiah 20:9)

I closed the door of my study, and for the next few minutes, I simply started talking into my phone. My mind wasn't overly engaged but the words flowed and poured forth without much effort or pause. In fact, I found myself speaking out about some things that I knew very little about.

The essence of the prophecy was that 2020 was going to be a very pivotal year. In fact, it would be the most significant of the past 50 years. I talked about how, like tectonic plates below the surface of the earth, the pressure had been building and would be released in early 2020. I described how political and racial tensions would boil over and there would be civil disorder in many cities across the States and that the National Guard would be called in to restore law and order. There was much more to this prophecy that many of you will have no doubt read.

At I concluded, honestly, I was a little stunned. I looked at what was written on my phone and, in my mind, I asked, *where did that come from?*

I live in Northern Ireland. A significant amount of this word was about the United States. I had heard of the National Guard but didn't actually know what they were. Plus, I knew that some of it sounded politically partisan. While I do have political leanings, I really had no desire to wade into the turbulent waters surrounding US politics.

The other thing that made me nervous was that this wasn't a particularly positive or overly encouraging word. At this stage, every other word I read about 2020 talked about '2020 vision' and how this would be the year of the 'double portion' and the 'best year of our lives'. My word spoke of significant geopolitical and spiritual sifting and shifting, turmoil, and turbulence.

The next question I asked myself was, *what am I to do with this?*

It wasn't exactly a word that would fit into one of my little yellow boxes on Instagram. With some trepidation, I sent it out to my email list, which at that time had around 1500 subscribers. I also posted it on the Daily Prophetic Facebook page and sent it to a website called '365Prophetic.com'.

To say that the response was mixed would be an understatement. The word did immediately resonate with a number of people and confirmed what they were already sensing about the incoming year. However, many others weren't quite so enthusiastic. Some, thinking I was making a political statement, sent me angry messages and unsubscribed. Others found it simply too negative and also unsubscribed. It wasn't the uplifting and inspirational word they had wanted or expected as they entered a new year.

Then February and March came along. Covid-19 started to spread across the globe followed by shutdowns, social distancing, and economic decline. In the middle of this racial tensions intensified and boiled over following the death of George Floyd in May.

Now, as I write this in late September, we have witnessed months of riots and disorder. There is so much uncertainty and apprehension about the future.

In my prophetic word, I had written these words: "In late summer there will be a constitutional crisis". Strangely, just last week I realized it was late summer and no such crisis had occurred. And then, just this past weekend, on the brink of possibly the most significant election in modern American history, a justice of the Supreme Court has just passed. Newsweek magazine has just posted a headline warning of a "constitutional crisis".

(Just as an aside, in recent months, I have received numerous emails of apology from some of those who were angry at what I had shared. As they have watched 2020 unfold, they have found themselves referring back to that word many times.)

That was a long introduction to get to the point I want to make.

The only reason I had the courage to send out that prophetic word was because of the way it came forth. It was a spontaneous, almost ecstatic prophetic revelation. It wasn't how I most frequently receive words. Therefore, I knew it was most likely God. I couldn't have made it up even if I had tried.

As I reflected on this, it led me to explore the different ways verbal prophetic words emerge, come forth and are birthed in the human spirit. Just as we all have different prophetic personalities, so we will tend to have a primary way that we receive and release prophecy.

DRIPPING, BURDENS, AND BUBBLING

The Hebrew word "to prophesy" means "to flow forth." It carries with it the thought "to bubble forth like a fountain, to let drop, to lift up, to tumble forth, and to spring forth." The Greek word that is translated "prophesy" means "to speak for another." It expresses the idea of speaking for God or being God's spokesman. This reflects what we read in Ezekiel 33:7: "You will receive a message from My mouth, and give them warning from Me."

A prophet or prophetess then, is a spokesperson for God, one who hears the voice of the Holy Spirit and communicates the mind of God to others, most often in verbal or written form.

However, the Bible offers little detail about the way or process in the prophet **actually received** the specific revelation from God. We read many variations in Scripture of:
"The word of the Lord came to me…"

"The Lord spoke to...."
"The Spirit of the Lord spoke through..."
"The Lord said..."
"The voice of the Lord..."

While we aren't ever told precisely what these phrases mean, it does seem that prophecy is imparted in different ways to different people. The person receiving the word obviously recognized it was the voice of God. It was incontestable and undeniable. The message was absolute in authority and demanded a response.

The Old Testament uses several Hebrew terms to describe the various ways God imparted prophetic revelation to His people.

RAINDROPS OF REVELATION

First, there is *nataf*, which means "to drop like rain." This describes a slow, gentle process where the prophetic word comes upon us little by little and accumulates in our spirits over a period of time. It's almost like a sponge that gradually absorbs the 'raindrops' of the prophetic revelation of the Lord until they fill up and overflow.

When I first read this definition, it really resonated with me. Very often, in the beginning, I will receive a small fragment of a word. It could be a phrase I hear or a sense I have or a picture I see or a word I read. But I just know there's something in it. I can tell there's more to come. So, I'll write it down somewhere and probably leave it for a while. Over time - it could be minutes, hours or days - more words slowly begin to percolate through. It's almost as if the faintest outline of a sketch drawing starts to get filled out and colored in. This may involve going back to the same word four or five times and adding new insight and revelation as it comes forth. Then, there then comes a point where I know it's complete. The sponge is saturated, the container is full, the picture is finished. At that point, I release the word in the appropriate way.

DEEPLY BURDENED

The second Hebrew word is *massa*. This refers to the "hand of the Lord" that releases the "burden of the Lord." When God's hand comes upon us, He imparts something to us – a prophetic 'burden'. He deposits something into our spirits. We then carry that burden as a word or commission from Him for as long as it remains upon us.

For example, you may receive a deep prophetic burden relating to a particular moral or social issue such as abortion, trafficking, racism, fatherlessness, worldliness in the church, etc. While others might feel strongly about the subject, for you it is a calling, almost a crusade. You cannot rest or settle without doing something to make a difference. There is a supernatural enablement of grace, a Holy Spirit impartation, to prophesy and intercede into that area in a way you never could before.

BUBBLING AND FLOWING

Another Hebrew word for prophetic impartation is *nabiy*. It is the common word used in the Old Testament for prophesy. It means to "flow forth" or "bubble forth like a fountain." At its essence, it means to be a 'mouthpiece for God' as is expressed in Psalm 81: 10: "Open wide your mouth and I will fill it." You hear and then you speak.

That most closely describes what happened when I received my word about 2020. This type of word isn't so much formed as it's downloaded. It is direct and requires little interpretation or application. It simply needs to be communicated verbally or in written form. It can be difficult to write fast enough to get everything down on paper. That's why I have started to dictate most words into my phone.

Nabiy prophecy is also often described as an 'immediate unction.' It is unpremeditated. Like water gushing from a broken water main, so prophetic words burst forth from the prophet. I find it similar to speaking in tongues. While energized by the Holy Spirit, you still have control over your mouth and can start or stop at will. ("The spirits of prophets are subject to prophets." 1 Cor 14: 32) However, you aren't consciously forming the sentences in your mind. God is filling your mouth with His words. At times it flows quietly and evenly. At other times it is loud and intense.

It is what you most commonly find expressed in a church gathering when an individual stands up and spontaneously speaks a prophetic word. Normally it's not written or prepared beforehand. The prophetic person begins to speak and as they do, the word of the Lord flows from them.

ECSTATIC PROPHECY

The *nabiy* type of prophecy is similar to, but different from, what we might call 'ecstatic prophecy.' Stacey Campbell offers this definition: "Ecstatic prophecy is a form of prophecy in which the prophet is completely overtaken by the Holy Spirit - body, soul, and spirit - and prophesies almost as an oracle." In other words, the Holy Spirit possesses and controls the mind and mouth of the prophet. It is almost a trance-like experience.

Many people find the idea of ecstatic possession uncomfortable. It can seem frenzied and even pagan. Yet, when you think about it, we believe that individuals can be possessed and controlled by demonic spirits. So why shouldn't we expect the same from the Holy Spirit?

We find ecstatic prophetic clearly described in a number of places in Scripture. For example, in 1 Samuel 19: 23 we read: "Saul went to Naioth at Ramah. But the Spirit of God came even on him, and he walked along prophesying until he came to Naioth." In fact, some leading scholars would maintain that all of the Old Testament prophets were ecstatic prophets to varying degrees. It is also pointed out that on the day of Pentecost it would appear that the 120 disciples who spoke in tongues were exhibiting ecstatic behavior. The fire fell and they went out into the streets speaking in unknown tongues.

While not as common today, ecstatic prophecy is still one means through which God does speak through and to His people. In a sense, the prophet actually embodies the Word of the Lord as he or she is supernaturally empowered.

For me, the closest I have come to this type of experience is when I have been preaching. I particularly remember one occasion not long after I was ordained. I was preaching at our main Sunday service when something happened. It felt almost like an out of body experience. A powerful anointing fell upon me and it seemed as if I was no longer speaking my words, but His words. I still had control in one sense, but I had surrendered my mind and message to the Holy Spirit and He took over. The congregation was deeply moved and there was a profound sense that we had heard the *now* Word of the Lord. The theologically conservative Senior Pastor of the church described it afterward as 'divine unction'. How I would love to experience that every week!

At different times you will receive revelation from God in different ways. I most often receive *nataf* words that come like raindrops and form over time, normally a day or two. You may be someone who becomes deeply burdened about some issue or cause. You personally feel the weight of it in a way that most others don't. That burden pushes you to intercession and action. In a later chapter, we will explore prophetic intercession. Perhaps you are more inclined towards *nabiy* prophecy, where the word of the

Lord bubbles up inside you and as you start speaking, it flows forth.

As with all prophetic revelation, the key is in learning to become aware of how God is communicating with you. Pay attention to what you see, hear, feel, and sense. Are you unusually burdened about something? Does it feel as if something is stirring within you? Do you notice words or images and they stand out more than usual? With intention and practice, over time your spiritual sensitivity increases, and you instinctively and naturally start to perceive what God is saying as you go through your day. Once that happens, it will feel as if you've gone from watching a black and white TV to living life in 4K.

Practical Exercise: As you go about your day, paying attention to what is standing out. Notice what you're noticing. Think about what you're thinking about. Perceive what you're looking at. Examine what you're feeling – physically, emotionally, spiritually – throughout your day as you drive, work, have conversations, watch the news, read, etc. Become more conscious and aware of how God is trying to get your attention in 100 different ways.

If something stands out, write it down or dictate it into your phone. Think about it. Reflect on it. Look at what you've written and ask the Holy Spirit for Revelation. Explore what the Bible says about that word/theme. Put it all down on paper and you'll be amazed how, over time, a coherent, cohesive prophecy starts to form and develop.

DAY 20

PROPHETIC PRAYER: PART 1

"We can all pray prophetically. However, a prophetic intercessor is not only equipped with insight from the Spirit - the prophetic intercessor becomes the vessel through whom the Spirit Himself prays."

(Helen Calder)

Rees Howells was a British missionary to South Africa in the early 20th century. Deeply impacted by the Welsh revival, as a young man, he spent three hours each evening on his knees reading the Bible and listening for the voice of God. He would discern the mind and heart of God for a situation and then intercede persistently until the prayer was answered. Sometimes the breakthrough came in a matter of hours, at other times it took months of crying out to God.

On one occasion, when his friend Joe was dying, Howells heard the Lord say that within one month, he would be healed. Howells set his heart to intercede, even though Joe and the doctor were doubtful. He told Joe that in one month, after he was healed, they would send a letter home to his family to share the good news.

Then the Lord challenged Howells to send the letter in faith, declaring the victory based on God's word to him, even before its manifestation. He mailed the letter, and the next day the power of the Holy Spirit descended on Joe and he was healed on the spot.

By the time of the Second World War, Rees Howells had returned from the mission field and had established a Bible college in Wales. Many people believe that he and his team had a huge impact on the course of world history in his day. When Hitler's focus turned on Britain in 1940, very little stood in his way. If Britain was defeated, Europe would be completely conquered by the Nazis.

Howells and the young people at the Bible College of Wales committed themselves to contend for spiritual victory so that physical battles on the ground could be won. He never underestimated the significance of the spiritual battle in which they were engaged: "I want to know that the Holy Spirit is stronger than the devil in the Nazi system. This is the battle of the ages, and victory here means victory for millions of people."

As they daily labored in intercession and waiting before the Lord, the Holy Spirit would often reveal Hitler's strategies ahead of time to Howells and his group of prayer warriors. They would then pray specifically and with great authority, and Hitler's armies would be defeated. God used Rees Howells and the young people with him at the Bible College of Wales in a mighty way to shape international events and the destiny of nations through their prayers. The world was in crisis, and this company of prophetic intercessors was raised up to be part of the solution.

PRAYING GOD'S HEART

We have so far focused on the prophetic in its many and varying aspects. But how does prophecy connect and interact with prayer? Of course, we know that God often speaks to us as we pray. We may hear the whisper of the Spirit, receive a picture or vision, or be directed to take certain steps in faith and obedience.

However, prophetic prayer is more than that.

Prophetic prayer occurs when we pray with insights (prophetic revelation) received from the Holy Spirit. We ask God to show us what's on His heart and mind and then to lead us in what to pray for and how to pray for it. As we enter into agreement with Him, our prayers become incredibly powerful and effective.

Paul tells us that the Holy Spirit helps us when we pray:

"In the same way, the Spirit helps us in our weakness. We do not know what we ought to pray for, but the Spirit himself intercedes for us through wordless groans. And he who searches our hearts knows the mind of the Spirit, because the Spirit intercedes for God's people in accordance with the will of God." (Rom 8:26-27)

The word *intercede* comes from two Latin words *inter* (between, among) and *cedere* (to go, to move, to yield, to pay a price). An intercessor, therefore, is a go-between, someone who steps into the gap when needed. They get involved in solving a problem.

Prophetic Intercession is a combination of intercession and prophecy. We are co-laboring with God to bring forth that which is true in the Spirit into the realm of the natural.

First, we want to know what God thinks about any situation we're praying about. This involves waiting upon the Lord, asking Him questions, tuning into His heart. As we listen, He imparts His desires, warnings, concerns, and promises to us. We then pray from that place of insight and revelation.

If we know what God already says about a matter, we can enter into agreement with Him with a great amount of authority and boldness. Our prayers become powerful and potent intercessions. With God agreeing, He has already said, "yes" to our request.

James Goll puts it like this:

"Prophetic intercession is the ability to receive a prayer request from God and pray it back to Him. God's hand comes on you, and He imparts His burden to you. Prophetic intercession is not as much *praying to God* as it is *praying with God.*"

It has often been said that not all intercessors are prophets, however, all prophets are called to intercede. And in the Bible, we see specific examples of those in a prophetic office who took time to intercede for those people and situations they ministered into. Moses intercedes for Israel (Exodus 34:8-9), Daniel for the Jews (Daniel 9:3-19), Jeremiah for Jerusalem (Jeremiah 14:20-21) and Elijah prayed for the drought he prophesied to begin and end (James 5:17-18). In the New Testament, Anna is an example of a prophetic intercessor. She poured years into her God-given assignment of praying in the temple, leading up to Jesus the Messiah's birth (Luke 2:36-38).

THE PRIVILEGE OF PARTNERING WITH HEAVEN

For many believers, prayer is a struggle. We want to pray. We know we ought to pray. We even know that prayer is incredibly powerful. And yet, many of us live prayerless lives.

Often out of a sense of guilt, we resolve to pray more. We set the alarm for an hour earlier in the morning. We write out prayer lists. We plan prayer walks. We start a journal. Then, ten minutes into our time with God, our minds start to wander. We pray through our list and aren't sure what else to do. We fall asleep. We don't see answers and grow discouraged.

How do we move beyond sheer willpower and discipline to where we begin to see prayer as a privilege and a delight?

I believe this happens as we begin to pray from a place of revelation rather than obligation. Prayer is primarily birthed out of intimacy with the Father. It is a dialogue, not a monologue. We listen to God, hear what is on His heart, and partner with Him in our prayers. We release Heaven's will here on earth. We declare out loud what God is saying about a situation. We join with angels in bringing to birth the purposes of God in our communities and cities. We prophetically decree the will of God over a region.

Then, we begin to see real change and significant transformation all around us. We realize that we have been given the keys of the Kingdom. What we bind on earth is bound in heaven and what we loose on earth is loosed in heaven (Matthew 16:19, 18:18). We understand that we are seated with Christ in the Heavenly realms (Ephesians 2:6) and so we can pray from His perspective. As we align our words with His will, we see results, and that motivates and inspires us to keep praying.

Prayer then becomes a privilege that we *get* to do, not a duty that we *have* to do. As Cindy Jacobs says: "Partnering in prayer with God is one of the greatest honors and privileges bestowed upon believers in Christ Jesus. Prayer changes things. Praying with God's heart moves mountains, calls forth the prophetic destiny upon a generation and brings you closer to the heart of God Himself!"

SIGNS YOU ARE A PROPHETIC INTERCESSOR

While every believer is called to engage in prophetic intercession, there are certain individuals who are specifically called to and anointed for this ministry. My wife is one of them. She hears from God and then prays with a passion and an authority that, honestly, makes me feel guilty at times. I often go out for an evening to a church meeting and when I come home after three hours, I'll ask Becky, "So, what did you do all evening?" Her answer invariably is, "I prayed." At this stage I've learned to stop asking, "Yes, but what else did you do?" She doesn't go around calling herself a prophetic intercessor, but that is definitely a part of her calling.

How do you know if you're specifically called and anointed for prophetic intercession? See if you can relate to any of the following:

- **You place a high value on hearing God when you pray.** You understand the importance of listening. Your first instinct in prayer is to seek the Lord for a prayer strategy. You press in to receive revelation from the Holy Spirit concerning *what* to pray and *how* to pray.

- **You tend to pray more at times when you feel urged by the Holy Spirit** (you may know this as a 'burden' of prayer). This isn't often necessarily in response to what you see or hear in the natural. Rather you sense an urgency in the Spirit, and you have to stop whatever you're doing to intercede.

- **Prayer is easier for you when you sense that the Holy Spirit has given you a specific burden or assignment.** However, you find it harder to pray when people assign prayer to you as a task, or give you lists and times to pray. You feel stifled and constricted as you prefer to be led by the Spirit.

- **You willingly give yourself over to travail** - a sense of birthing the purposes of God - and you may have experienced wordless groans or weeping in your prayer times. You cannot decide to go into travail. It is a work of the Holy Spirit within you and through you. But you can choose to resist it or submit and yield to it. In this, you can identify with Hannah (1 Samuel 1:10-13) and Elijah - who prayed for rain in the birthing position (1 Kings 18:41-44).

- **When you have a prayer assignment, it may feel as though you are personally involved and invested in the situation.** You may have a sense of identification in the Spirit with those you are praying for. You may feel what they are feeling, or sense God's heart towards them, such as compassion, grief, or mercy.

- **You do not always need to have specific knowledge about what you are praying for.** Sometimes you pray in the realm of 'mystery' (1 Cor 14:2). It is enough for you to know that the Spirit has called you to prayer.

- **You may be sent by God to certain places or people at particular times to intercede on behalf of a situation, person, or region.** You may not even know why you are going or what you'll do when you get there, but you move in response to the leading of the Holy Spirit.

- **You have a strong sense of intimacy with the Holy Spirit when you pray - and this fuels your prayer life.** You know the 'secret place' of prayer. Your prayer life is often hidden, and sometimes not understood or appreciated by people. However, your reward is found in the presence of God.

- **You experience a deep sense of satisfaction in prayer**, especially in being at the right place, at the right time for your God-given assignment to pray on behalf of a person, group, region, or situation.

As you read through these, did many resonate with you? If so, you may well be someone who has the grace of prophetic intercession upon your life. Press into it. Study it further. Align yourself with others who have a similar calling. Above all, listen and pray!

Perhaps you didn't connect with many of the above statements. That's totally okay too. Honestly, I don't find myself particularly drawn to this ministry. Of course, I place a high value on both prayer and the prophetic. But I'm not graced to spend hours laboring in intercession or travail. Yet, I do want to pray with increased power and effectiveness. I long to see more answered prayer. I want to use the spiritual authority I have been given to break strongholds and release all of the resources of Heaven.

With that in mind, I encourage you to spend more time listening when you pray. Seek God's strategies in relation to *what* you pray for and *how* you pray. Nothing will fuel your prayer life more than seeing situations shift and circumstances change in response to your prophetic prayers.

Practical Exercise: I would encourage you to pray that God would reveal His heart to you as you begin, or continue on, your journey of prophetic prayer:

Father, in the mighty name of the Son of God, I ask that You bring my heart into union with Yours so that it can bear with the burdens and desires that are in Your heart. Give me both an increase of the Spirit of revelation and the supernatural authority to stand in the gap in the name of Jesus. I want to pray Your prophetic promises into being. Amen.

DAY 21

PROPHETIC PRAYER: PART 2

"Many times, we are waiting on God to do something, and He is waiting on us to pray prophetic prayers as we release our faith, so that He can manifest His purposes in and through us."

(Kynan Bridges)

Several years ago, God spoke to both my wife and I that we were going to receive "a large lump sum" of money. That was the exact phrase we both heard – "a large lump sum".

I grew up in a lower-middle-class family so, for me, a large lump sum is anything over $1000. At the time, I prayed into this word and sensed God speak to me about a very specific amount that we were going to receive. Honestly, this figure was so large that it had to come from God! I would never have come up with a number that big on my own.

I wrote the figure down in my prayer diary and began to, almost daily, declare over my life: "Thank you God for giving us ___." However, I only had a number. I didn't know if it was going to be in Euros or Pounds Sterling. (We were living in Dublin at the time which uses Euros. However, in Northern Ireland, where we both are from, the currency is Sterling.) So, I just quoted the number to God, and prophetically declared that it was mine.

Six months passed and no money appeared.

Then, out of the blue, someone gave us a gift of 3000 euros for a family vacation. While I was overwhelmed by their generosity, that amount fell well short of the "large lump sum" that I had originally heard from the Father.

So, I continued to prophetically pray: "Thank you God for giving us ____."

Then Becky's grandfather sadly passed. He had been shrewd with finances, so honestly, we both thought that perhaps the money would come from his will.

We didn't receive a penny, God rest his soul!

I continued to declare this "large lump sum" over my life.

For over 14 months, I prayerfully and prophetically declared the exact figure God had spoken to me, thanking God as if it had already happened. Then, one Sunday, a businessman from the States who I had only met a few times previously, attended our church in Dublin. He was in Ireland for a few days visiting family.

Following the service, we went for lunch. As we were waiting for our food to be served, he said: "Craig, you need a sabbatical. God spoke to me during the service and told me that I should pay for it. Here's what I'm going to give you." He then quoted the EXACT amount of money God had spoken to me about all those months before. I wept at the dinner table. When I returned home, I shared the news with my wife. She cried also. Then we both laughed and jumped around the room praising God for His faithfulness and goodness!

SPEAKING GOD'S PROMISES

We have been learning that prophetic intercession involves hearing God's word and will and then praying it into fulfillment and fruition. It is a very targeted and focussed type of prayer, fixed on a specific outcome. Rather than saying, "Thy will be done", we take the time to discern what the Father's will is before we pray. Then we can intercede with boldness and authority, knowing that we are already aligned with His heart.

This may happen in a corporate gathering, such as a church prayer meeting. It can also be part of your personal prayer life, as the above example from my own recent experience demonstrates.

In fact, for about 20 years now, I have spoken, decreed, and declared God's Word, promises, favor, and blessing over every area and aspect of my life.

Most days I simply say: *"I declare God's favor over my family. I speak God's blessing over my marriage... finances... health... ministry..."*

When, God has spoken specifically to me about something, as He did with the "large lump sum", I keep on speaking His promise until I see it.

Has my life perfect? Of course not.

Have I experienced God's blessing and favor in abundance? Absolutely!

The seeds of continually prophetically declaring God's favor over my life have, over time, grown, budded, and blossomed.

I'm always very aware that this could be construed as being 'new-age' metaphysics or the 'confess it and possess it' doctrine at the extreme end of the 'prosperity Gospel'. I don't believe that to be the case. I am simply taking seriously what the Scriptures teach about the power of God's Word, the power of our words, and the spiritual authority we, as believers, possess in Christ.

YOUR WORDS HAVE POWER

Earlier in this book, we saw how God created men and women in His image and likeness. The Creator actually breathed into us His divine nature and life. In the early chapters of Genesis, we read again and again: "God said…and there was…" His words have absolute authority and creative power. As creatures made to reflect His nature, so our words also carry significant authority and power. Obviously not anywhere close to the same degree and measure as God's words. Nonetheless, as redeemed spiritual/physical beings, we should be careful not to underestimate the amount of authority God has delegated to His children.

In Matthew 10, when Jesus sent out the twelve, he "gave them authority to drive out impure spirits and to heal every disease and illness." (v. 1) In other words, Jesus imparted some of His own authority over the invisible realm to His followers.

Following His death and resurrection, He sent out His followers into the world with these words:

"All authority in heaven and on earth has been given to me. Therefore go and make disciples…" (Matthew 20: 18-19)

I believe God is absolutely sovereign. We can never manipulate or force Him to do anything. However, in His sovereignty, God has willingly chosen to delegate a significant amount of His authority to His people here on earth to demonstrate His Kingdom, enforce His rule and overcome the enemy. Therefore, the words we speak, when aligned with His will, are infused with Divine power and creative potential. Never underestimate the power of speaking God's Word and prophetically declaring His will over your life, situations and circumstances. The Bible is very clear: "The tongue has the power of life and death…" (Proverbs 18: 21)

PRAYING THE SCRIPTURES

God's written Word, the Bible, is like no other book. Over many centuries, men (and possibly women) were prompted and inspired by the Holy Spirit to write down the character and commands of Yahweh, the utterances of His prophets, the ministry of His Son, and the life of His people. His Word contains His promises and principles, His desires and decrees, His works and ways. Paul told his protégé, Timothy, that "All Scripture is God-breathed…". The book of Hebrews also makes it clear that "the word of God is alive and active." (4: 12) The Bible has supernatural power in its pages.

When faced with a problem, search the Word until you find a promise. Pray the Scriptures over your life, family, church, community, and the nations. When you do this, you are always praying according to God's will. Psalm 138: 2 says "You have exalted above all things your name and your word." God will back up His Word because His name is at stake. As the late Reinhard Bonnke once said: "God's Word in our mouth is just as powerful as God's Word in His own mouth".

This can be as simple as reading Scripture out loud. It may also involve personally proclaiming His promises over your life. For example, if anxious about finances, I might say something like:

"Thank you, Lord, that your Word tells me not to be anxious but to bring my petitions and requests to you. I declare that you are my Shepherd, therefore I lack nothing. I have confidence that You, my God, shall supply all of my needs according to Your riches in Christ Jesus. As I have given, so shall it be given to me - good measure, pressed down, shaken together, and running over. Thank you that you will God will generously provide all that I need. Not only that, but I will always have everything I need and plenty left over to share with others. I receive Your peace and your provision. In Jesus' name. Amen."

God's Word is eternal, it is always relevant, and, as a believer, you can pray and declare it over your situation and circumstances and see things shift. Call your world to align with His Word.

PROCLAIMING PROPHETIC PROMISES

Have you ever received a prophetic word that you knew was from God, yet it hasn't been fulfilled? I think most of us have had that experience. There are a few things we need to understand.

Firstly, when God gives you a prophetic word, He is speaking from your future into your present. He is calling you forward to become all He has made you to be and to do all He has purposed you to do. That word is filled with the potential of what is possible in your life.

However, a response is required on your part. Many people receive a word and become passive, almost displaying an attitude of: "If God said it, then it's going to happen no matter what I do." That is not how it works. Every word requires an appropriate response from you.

We see this throughout the Bible. God told His people that He had brought them out of Egypt to bring them into the Promised Land.

However, because of their disobedience, idolatry, and grumbling, a whole generation died in the wilderness and never inherited the promise.

In 1 Samuel 13: 13, the prophet tells Saul: "You have not kept the command the LORD your God gave you; if you had, he would have established your kingdom over Israel for all time." Think about that.
God is basically saying: "If you would have done this, then I would have done that." Saul's disobedience forfeited him from receiving the fullness of all God had planned for him.

We always have a part to play in taking hold of all that God wants to give us. It may require an act of faith, a season of preparation, patience, a demonstration of obedience, moving location, sacrifice, or dealing with some character issues. As we partner with God, He shows us the steps we need to take to enter into the fulfillment of His promises.

We also need to understand that, once a prophetic word is released over your life, very often the enemy will immediately come against that word and try to rob it from you. Have you ever received a prophecy and within days your life looks like the complete opposite of what was spoken over you? In Matthew 13, in the Parable of the Sower, Jesus talked about how "the evil one comes and snatches away what was sown" and "trouble or persecution comes because of the word". In other words, the enemy immediately tries to abort the prophetic word at its seed stage, before it even has a chance to germinate. Therefore you will often need to contend for what God has said through bold prayer, prophetic decrees, and spiritual warfare.

In 1 Timothy 1: 18, Paul says:

"Timothy, my son, I am giving you this command in keeping with the prophecies once made about you, so that by recalling them you may fight the battle well…"

Paul tells Timothy to "recall" the prophetic words spoken over his life and to wield them as weapons of warfare against the enemy.

So, at the beginning of this chapter, I shared how God spoke to me about a specific "lump sum" of money. What I didn't tell you was that in the next 12 months, we went through the most difficult year financially we have ever experienced as a family. My wife is a speech pathologist and has never been without work. However, during this time, due to a lack of funding, her contract wasn't renewed. We were living in Dublin which is one of the most expensive cities in Europe. Plus we incurred some unplanned expenses such as medical bills and car repairs. Everything seemed to go against the prophetic word that God was going to bless us financially. Yet, as I held firmly to what God had said and kept declaring it out loud as if it was already done, we saw breakthrough and blessing.

Have you given up on something God has spoken to you because of opposition, obstacles, adversity, or weariness? Perhaps it's time to dust off those prophetic words and begin to daily declare them over your life.

DECLARING YOUR DESIRES

This last aspect of prophetic prayer is the one that makes people most nervous. Yet, I feel as if I would be withholding one of the most powerful secrets that God has shown me over the past 20 years if I didn't share it with you.

What are we to do with those dreams and desires in our hearts where we can't find an obvious verse or promise in Scripture and God hasn't spoken to us about it prophetically? I believe that as long as we aren't disobeying God's Word or going against what we know to be His will, we have permission to speak, decree, and declare those things over and into our lives.

Psalm 37: 4 says:

"Take delight in the LORD, and he will give you the desires of your heart."

Most of us have no problem with the first part of that verse. We want to delight in the Lord and find our deepest joy and satisfaction in Him. However, when it comes to "the desires of our hearts", we begin to struggle a little. What if my desires aren't God's will? Or, what if my desires are selfish? What if I'm just being ambitious, greedy, and prideful?

My response would be: why would you assume that your desires aren't also God's desires for you? He formed you in the womb and wired you with your unique personality and needs. Plus, the fact that you're even concerned about being out of the will of God or being selfish is almost a guarantee that you won't be. The Lord is well able to direct the submissive heart.

These desires that I'm talking about here could be anything from longing for a spouse to wanting to be debt-free to dreaming of owning a house by the sea. Just because the desire isn't to eradicate world hunger and rescue children from trafficking doesn't make it wrong.

I personally have a prayer list of desires which I speak over my life regularly. One of those that I added last year would be that Becky would sell the house that she purchased in 2007 at the peak of the market, just before the financial crash. The monthly repayments have been an annoyance, if not a burden, our entire married life.

Was this desire something that would make a difference to anyone else but us? No. Could we survive without the house being sold? Yes. But it was still a legitimate desire of both our hearts and it wasn't contrary to God's Word.
So, for months I have declared: "Becky has sold her house for more than she currently owes." As I write this today, Becky has just returned from signing the papers and the sale will be completed later this week.

In the Old Testament, David told God that he wanted to build a temple to honor Yahweh, his God. This desire was birthed in David's heart, not God's heart. Look at what we read:

"David said to Solomon: "My son, I had it in my heart to build a house for the Name of the LORD my God. But this word of the LORD came to me: '…You are not to build a house for my Name…But you will have a son…He is the one who will build a house for my Name. He will be my son, and I will be his father.

And I will establish the throne of his kingdom over Israel forever." (1 Chronicles 22: 7-10)

Isn't that beautiful? God says: "I love that this desire was in your heart. But you're not the one to do it. Instead, your son will do it and I'll lavish him with blessing forever."

As a dad, I want to meet my child's needs. But even more than that, I love to watch him flourish and thrive in every area of life as he understands who he is and what his passions are. I want to resource his dreams. I love to see his face light up when I give him something that he really wants but doesn't necessarily need. Plus, I also know when to withhold something if I believe it's not best for him, no matter how much he wants it.

As Jesus said: "If you, then, though you are evil, know how to give good gifts to your children, how much more will your Father in heaven give good gifts to those who ask him!" (Matthew 7: 11)

He really is a good, good Father.

Start to pray His Word, proclaim prophetic promises, and declare your desires. If you will do this consistently, you will be amazed at how your life begins to align with your words.

Practical Exercise: What is in your heart? What are your dreams and desires? What do you long to see in your life? Could these also possibly be things that God would love to give you?

Write them down. Be honest and be specific. Speak them over your life as if you already have them. Let God refine and reshape them. I always find it incredible as I come back to my list in six months or a year later just to see how many of my dreams and desires have been fulfilled.

DAY 22

PROPHETIC WISDOM: GIVING PROPHETIC WORDS

"The answer to abuse is not non-use but correct use."
(Arthur Wallis)

Early in my ministry, a young couple who were members of the church I was leading, experienced three miscarriages within a short space of time. As you can imagine, they were devastated by these losses. They took their toll physically, emotionally, and spiritually. As I counseled them, I recommended that they hold off on trying to have a child for a little while, just to give them both time to heal. I was concerned about the effects that another miscarriage might have on them.

Around four weeks later, one morning, in that in-between time when you're not asleep but not yet fully awake, I had a short vision. In the picture, the wife in this couple was sitting up in a bed in the maternity ward of a hospital, nursing a healthy baby boy. It was brief but very vivid. I sensed it was from the Lord.

What would you do here in my position? Probably, like me, you'd want to tell the couple what you'd seen. But what if I was wrong? What if she didn't get pregnant again? Or if she had another miscarriage?

This is where prophetic wisdom is required.

Earlier in this book I wrote that prophecy has three different components or aspects:

- **Revelation**: *What is God saying? What do you see, sense, hear?*

- **Interpretation**: *What does it mean? It's almost like translating God's language to yours.*

- **Application**: *What am I supposed to do with it? What does this practically mean?*

In this case, the revelation was the vision itself.
The interpretation seemed fairly straightforward. The lady was going to have a healthy baby boy.
What about the application? Why did God show me this? What did He want me to do with it?

As I sought His direction, I really sensed that I wasn't to share this word with the couple. The Lord wanted me to pray them through the pregnancy, interceding for the unborn child as it gestated and grew in the womb to full-term.

Later, on the same day as I had received this vision, I had lunch with the Senior Pastor I was serving under. I mentioned the couple and he immediately responded: "They were actually in touch earlier today. Julie (not her real name) is pregnant again."

I shared my vision with him and he agreed that I should keep in touch with them and continue to pray, without mentioning the prophetic revelation.

I vividly remember the afternoon I walked into the maternity ward of the local hospital, and there, sitting up in the bed, was this young mother, proudly holding her healthy, newborn son. As I later exited the room, she called after me: "Craig, you knew all along we were going to have a boy, didn't you? Thank you for your prayers."

THE PITFALLS OF PROPHECY

Of all the spiritual gifts, prophecy is the one that is most open to misuse and abuse. When someone walks up to you and says, "God told me….", it can be very difficult to argue with them. If you disagree, are you going against the will of God? I could tell you countless stories of people who genuinely believed that God told them to do all sorts of ridiculous, unhelpful, and even sinful things.

Because of such abuses and silliness, many churches avoid permitting the exercise of the prophetic gift altogether. They have perhaps been burned in the past and it seems safer just to shut the operation of this ministry, rather than risk further damage. While I understand their caution, when it is used properly, with wisdom and within Biblical boundaries, prophecy is so incredibly helpful and effective in building up churches and bringing direction from the Holy Spirit.

In this chapter, I want to offer some practical wisdom to help you share prophetic words and other revelation without causing harm to others or ourselves.

THE 'DO'S' OF PROPHECY

DO BE PART OF A LOCAL CHURCH: In 30 years of following Jesus, I have become very wary of prophets and ministers who aren't connected to some local church. The itinerant preacher/prophet who is accountable to no one but God can be dangerous and often deceived. Everyone in authority should also be submitted to Godly, spiritual authority. At this stage, I simply will not permit anyone to preach/minister in our church unless they are under the covering of a church family.

DO BE HUMBLE: The purpose of any spiritual gift is to serve others, not to build your personal platform or draw attention to yourself. Sadly, over time, those who are gifted can start to believe the compliments of others and develop delusions of grandeur. Keep people around you who help you remain grounded. And always remember that it is a *gift* – you did nothing to earn it or deserve it.

DO BE BIBLICAL: I know we covered this earlier, but so much damage could be avoided if prophetic people simply stayed within the parameters of Scripture. Read your Bible, meditate on its words, and when you prophesy, try to saturate your words in Scripture. It will carry so much more power and authority. And, of course, never say anything contrary to the clear teaching of God's Word. That's called heresy.

DO BE TEACHABLE: This goes along with remaining humble but also involves finding people who are further along in using their gift and seeking to learn from them. In writing this book, I have turned to around 30 other books covering all aspects of prophetic ministry. Especially with those areas which are new to me, the wisdom and experience of others have been invaluable.

Also, submit to the leadership of your local church. If you give a word and they tell you it was a little 'off', don't become defensive or reactive. Simply listen and learn so that you can grow and develop. As a pastor, I watch very closely how people receive correction. Someone who is genuinely humble and teachable is also promotable. Someone with a proud heart or defensive attitude isn't going to be entrusted with any level of leadership or responsibility.

DO BE WILLING TO MAKE MISTAKES: If you are genuinely taking risks and sharing what you sense God is saying, you will get it wrong at times. It can be embarrassing and affect your confidence in using your gift. However, please don't give up. It is only by practice that you will grow and develop in recognizing God's voice.

Earlier this year, there was a huge march planned for Washington DC. For days I felt unusually burdened that there was going to be a planned and concerted attempt to breach the perimeter of the White House and begin an insurrection. With much hesitation, I shared this word on my Instagram page. It turned out I was wrong. The crowd was many times smaller than had been estimated and dispersed without major incident. Some would say that the crisis was averted because of prayer. Perhaps so. I'd rather just put my hands up and say that I got it wrong.

The Bible says that "we know in part and we prophesy in part" (1 Corinthians 13:9). Not only are we sometimes wrong, but we are seldom totally right. None of us really see the whole picture, but only 'in part'. Even the most gifted prophets in the world can miss it at times or misinterpret what they receive. It keeps us humble, teachable, and fully dependent on the Lord.

DO TIME IT RIGHT: Just because you have received a revelation, doesn't mean it has to be shared in the next five minutes. You can give the right word at the wrong time and it falls flat (or even worse, does harm).

If it is really from the Holy Spirit, you will likely remember it. (Or you can simply write it down, just in case.) The Bible says that "The spirits of prophets are subject to the control of prophets" (1 Corinthians 14: 32). In other words, you have control over your mouth. This is especially true in a church gathering where you can completely disrupt the flow of the service if you interrupt with your 'urgent' prophetic word.

In one of our services, a man once stood up during my sermon and began to prophesy to the congregation. While I recognized him, he wasn't a member of our church. I politely asked him to sit down and speak to me later. Undeterred, he continued to speak. I then asked him with more force to sit down immediately. He kept going. At that point, I told him I would have him removed from the building if he continued to speak. He sat down.

DO ASK FOR PERMISSION: Be very careful not to violate someone's privacy or personal space. Before you prophesy over someone, ask for their permission, especially if you don't know them or others are listening in. Simply say: "I think God wants to speak to you. Would it be okay if I shared what I sense He is saying?" Also, don't ever place your hands on someone without first asking for their permission. It's courteous and avoids all sorts of awkward situations.

DO KEEP LISTENING TO THE HOLY SPIRIT: As you are sharing prophetically with someone, there will come a point where the flow of the utterance naturally stops. At that point, don't keep talking! Simply remain in God's presence, asking the Father if there is anything else He wants to say. Very often you will receive additional revelation if you will take the time to listen.

DO BE YOURSELF: We all have preachers and prophets who we are naturally drawn to. We perhaps like their style or charisma. While we can learn from them, don't mimic them. I have watched too many people trying to preach like Bill Johnson or prophesy like Shawn Bolz. Just be yourself. God doesn't need another Bill Johnson, Shawn Bolz, Steven Furtick, or TD Jakes. But he does want you to fully express all that He has placed inside you.

On that note, use your normal voice and language when delivering a prophetic word. Avoid a dramatic tone or and don't use King James English i.e. "Thus saith the Lord....". Be conversational while being attentive to any emphasis the Spirit is giving to particular words or phrases.

DO BE AWARE OF YOUR OWN BIASES, WOUNDS AND EMOTIONS: You can be both highly anointed and deeply wounded at the same time. The prophetic revelation you release flows through the filter of your humanity. If you are carrying unresolved hurts, resentment, or prejudice, that will taint what you share with others. For example, if you are ministering to someone who looks very similar to a person who betrayed you in the past, you may end up prophesying out of that association, not from the Spirit. If you are feeling angry about a situation, you may unintentionally use prophecy to vent your anger. If you are overly tired, take a break. It is better to excuse yourself than to misuse your gift.

Examine your heart and motives constantly when you are exercising the gift. Like David, pray every day: "Create in me a clean heart." (Psalm 51: 10)

THE 'DON'TS' OF PROPHECY

DON'T SAY: "GOD TOLD ME…" There is rarely a week that passes that I don't receive an email or direct message where someone says something like: "God told me to share this with you", or, "God told me you had a word for me." The only problem is that God didn't tell me! When we are commanded not to "use the Lord's

name in vain", that means more than just saying 'OMG'. It is also attributing God's name onto something that He clearly did not say.

Even when prophesying, be very careful of saying: "God told me…" That removes the human element which is always there and makes it difficult to dispute whatever you say next. It is so much better, especially in the early stages of developing this gift to say something like: "I sense that God might be saying to you…." or, "I feel the Lord might be indicating…."

After I have shared a prophetic word, I will almost always ask: "Does that make sense to you?" If it does, great. If not, simply say: "That's okay. Sure why don't you write it down and keep it on the shelf in case at some stage in the future it becomes relevant."

DON'T GIVE DIRECTIVE PROPHECY: This would include prophesying births, deaths, marriages, house moves, or major financial decisions. The complexities and potential for problems around this caution should be obvious. On the very rare occasions where God does speak to you very clearly about one of these issues, make sure there is accountability and a witness present.

It goes without saying that you should never pressurize anyone into following a prophetic word. This is especially the case in matters of the heart. Many sincere believers have 'heard God say' that they were going to marry a particular individual. Again, the only problem is that God hasn't told the other person the same thing. One writer calls this prophetic "wishions". They come packaged as a vision but are really only wishful thinking.

DON'T EVER MANIPULATE: It is possible to use your prophetic gift to manipulate others into agreeing with you or to control others through convincing them that your words are the very words of God Himself.

Also, those with a proven gift of prophecy sometimes know things about people and situations which they could use to their own advantage if they so desired.

There are even some 'prophets' today who charge money to give prophetic words. I believe that those in full-time ministry should be adequately compensated and if someone wants to give a donation/gift to a ministry, that's a good thing. But to charge a $50 fee for a two-minute prophetic word is shameful and brings the gift into disrepute.

Don't ever use your gift to manipulate or control others, or from a place of greed. It is to be used to serve others, and for their benefit, not for your personal gain.

DON'T BE HARSH: Be extremely cautious about prophesying about particular sins or revealing information that could cause division or damage relationships. Always submit the information to a mature Christian leader before you share it any further. Prophecy is intended to build up and strengthen, not to tear down and destroy.

Occasionally God will give prophetic people words of rebuke or correction for others. They are always to be spoken in grace, with a heart that longs to see repentance and restoration, not judgment.

We have already mentioned the tone in which you speak. How you give a prophetic word is often as important as the content that you share. Do you look and sound like Jesus as you are speaking to them? Is this how you would like to be spoken to? Tenderness, grace and kindness in your demeanor can make even the most difficult words easier to receive.

DON'T RUSH TO INTERPRET THE REVELATION: When God gives you a word or picture for someone, the temptation is to try to figure out what it means and apply it to their lives. Almost without exception, all that God wants you to do is to share what He has shown you. You are the postman. You don't need to open and make sense of all the mail. Something that means absolutely nothing to you could be incredibly significant to the other person.

LEAVE THE RESULTS TO GOD

Once you have shared the prophetic word or revelation, your job is over – except to pray. If your advice is not taken, you shouldn't feel rejected or dishonored. Nor should you feel that those who refuse to listen to your admonition are hard-hearted or rebellious. Leave the results with God.

Also, as long as you have delivered it with care and without manipulation, you are not responsible for what people do based on a prophetic word you give to them. A few years ago I prophesied over a lady who was visiting our church. I didn't know her, but after the service she told me that the word was incredibly accurate. As a result of that prophecy, she consequently made several significant decisions. Later, when one of those decisions didn't work out as she had hoped, I received an angry email blaming me for what had gone wrong.

The truth is, I never told her what to do. I simply passed on what the Father showed me, and she interpreted it and applied it as she thought best at the time. Therefore, I carry absolutely no responsibility for what happened next.

I know that after reading this chapter some of you will be nervous and overly cautious about making mistakes. However, if the desire of your heart is genuinely to serve, encourage, and build up others, you can avoid so many of the problems and pitfalls of prophetic ministry. Remember, it's not about you. It's about revealing the heart of the Father to His children. Take the pressure off your performance and focus on developing your relationship with the Holy Spirit. He will lead, guide, and direct you into all truth.

Practical Exercise: While reading the above cautions, which one stood out as being most relevant and applicable to you? Write down what you are going to do to improve in that area?

DAY 23

PROPHETIC WISDOM: RECEIVING PROPHETIC WORDS

"God gives you a future-oriented prophetic word so that you will take hold of that and in faith pull it into your now."
(Graham Cooke)

During my teenage years, I received a significant number of prophetic words about my future. Through various men and women, in different settings, God spoke to me about leadership and ministry. One word in particular stands out. I was told that one day I would preach the Gospel before national leaders.

To my sixteen-year-old mind, at the time this seemed impossible. I wasn't from a wealthy or influential family. My parents weren't even believers. Plus, I really struggled with nerves, especially when speaking or reading in public. I wrote the prophecy in the back of my Bible and referred back to it now and again, always wondering how God could make such a thing happen.

Fast-forward 18 years. I had been in ordained ministry for four years when I had the privilege of leading a lady named Margaret from our congregation to faith in Christ. The incredible thing was that everyone assumed that Margaret was already a believer. At this stage in her early 60's, she had been in church her whole life, even holding various positions of responsibility. She was even the Christian chaplain of a women's organization. However, upon hearing a presentation of the Gospel, that we are saved by faith alone in Christ alone, Margaret realized that she had been relying upon her good works for salvation.

She was wonderfully saved and immediately people noticed a difference in her life. Her whole countenance seemed to soften and radiate Jesus.

Since childhood, Margaret had struggled with respiratory conditions and within a year of coming to faith, she went home to be with Jesus.

Here's the interesting part of the story. At the time of her death, Margaret's sister was serving her second term as the Mayor of our city. Therefore, Margaret's funeral was packed with almost 1000 people, many of them being national political leaders here in Northern Ireland. I stood before that large congregation and shared

Margaret's testimony, telling the crowd how she had come to saving faith through the Gospel of Jesus.

When I received that prophetic word 18 years before this, I could never have possibly imagined how it would come to pass. But God, who exists outside of time, had already seen into my future and declared over my life what would happen.

I RECEIVED A PROPHECY, WHAT DO I DO NOW?

In most churches, I've found that there are two groups of people when it comes to the prophetic. Some love receiving prophetic words. They tend to sit at the front when a prophet is in town and wear brightly colored neon shirts, hoping to get picked out and receive a word. Then there are those who slump down in their chair, trying to hide, praying that they aren't chosen.

I have to admit, I fall into the first category. I love receiving prophetic ministry. It has been so influential and impactful in my life for the past 30 years. If God has something to say, I want to hear it.

However, at times I have struggled with the words I have received. Some immediately felt 'off', others sounded incomprehensible or downright weird, and others haven't come to pass more than years later.

What do you do when you receive a prophetic word?

When God speaks into your life, how do you steward the prophecy and how can you discern what to do next?

How much of it is your responsibility and how much do you leave to God?

That's what we'll be exploring in this chapter.

THE NATURE OF A PROPHETIC WORD

Before we get into the practicalities, first we need to understand that **personal prophetic words are *partial*, *progressive*, and *conditional*.**

Partial: The Bible says that "we prophesy in part" (1 Corinthians 13: 9). A prophecy is just one small insight into God's will for our lives. It never contains the whole picture. God reveals what we need to know in order to help us do his will in a particular area, time, and place. At best, we are given a glimpse of a movie trailer, not the entire film. Or, to use another analogy, we are handed a peek into one short chapter of a book, but we don't know the rest of the story. There are some things that we don't need (or want) to know ahead of time.

For example, as a young man, Joseph had two dreams about his father and brothers bowing down to him. Those prophetic revelations were true and came to pass later in his life. However, Joseph wasn't shown all that would happen in-between. There were no dreams about the pit, palace, or prison.

Understanding that prophecy always reveals only a part of God's will for our lives keeps us from despairing when a prophecy fails to mention a specific area of concern. Just because God says nothing about it, doesn't mean it's not going to happen.

Progressive: Prophecy unfolds progressively and expands gradually over the years. Often new prophetic revelation adds another piece to the overall picture. We might be shown the next step to take or even what the destination looks like, but we are not given the entire map. It is only through a daily walk of faith and obedience that we step into the good future God has planned for us.

We see this exemplified in the life of Abraham. At around the age of 50, God speaks to him about leaving his country and going to a land He would show him. Over the next 75 years, God spoke to him at different times about his offspring, and more specifically, his son Isaac.

Conditional vs. Unconditional Prophecy: There are certain things God decrees which will come to pass no matter how humans respond. No power of hell or scheme of man can stop them. These are usually more general prophecies about the bigger picture of human history rather than personal prophecies directed to individuals.

For example, Daniel prophetically interpreted Nebuchadnezzar's dream as predicting the rise and fall of several empires. This was God's predestined purpose and nothing could stop it.

Conditional prophecies, on the other hand, are prophetic words and revelations where the fulfillment is dependent upon human response. They can be canceled, altered, reversed, or diminished. For the prophecy to come to pass, requires the proper participation and cooperation of the one who receives the prophetic word.

Understanding the conditional nature of prophecy is vital if we are to walk into God's will and ways for our lives. Most of us know people who, at some stage in their lives, received great prophetic words about their future. Today many of them aren't even walking with Christ.

Even in our own lives, we sometimes have a very passive and 'que sera sera, whatever will be will be' attitude about prophetic words we receive. We presume that if God said it, automatically it's going to happen, no matter what we do. This is a fallacy and leads many into delay or disappointment as they wait and wait for God to fulfill His word.

In Exodus 6, God declared "I will" to Moses seven times, with regards to Israel's liberation and possession of Canaan. Yet, these prophetic promises were fulfilled for only two of the men who were alive when they were given. Because of their disobedience, idolatry, and grumbling, the rest of the Israelite population never entered into what God had spoken over them.

We can also look at the life of Saul. He was anointed by Samuel to be the King of Israel. However, because of his people-pleasing, pride, and insecurity, he disobeyed God and forfeited what God had planned for him. Look at what God says to him:

"You have not kept the command the LORD your God gave you; if you had, he would have established your kingdom over Israel for all time. But now your kingdom will not endure…"
(1 Samuel 13: 13-14)

While Saul was allowed to remain in his position as King for another 15 to 20 years, the Holy Spirit had departed from him and the prophetic promises had been annulled in his life and transferred onto David.

When we receive personal prophetic words today, we need to understand that they are partial, progressive, and conditional. Only as we cooperate with the Lord, can we expect to see the fulfillment of what He has spoken to us.

So, how do we respond properly to prophecy? Here's some practical wisdom I think will be helpful.

HANDLING PROPHETIC WORDS

Be open to God speaking through different people in various ways. At times, I have received significant prophetic words through people I didn't even know had a prophetic gifting. Sometimes God will even speak through people we don't like!

Don't reject the word because you aren't enamored with the vessel it comes through.

Always record prophetic words. If you can, use your phone to record the prophecy as it is spoken over you. If not, write down as much of it as you can remember, as soon as possible. Even if at the time it didn't make a lot of sense, years later you might be amazed as you look back and see old words come to pass. Recording prophecies also helps you to compare them and identify patterns of what God might be speaking over your life.

Read your prophecies regularly. This is obviously contingent upon you following through with the previous point. I have found it helpful to go back to the words spoken over my life and examine what has already come to pass and what am I still waiting to see fulfilled. It's good to remind yourself of what God has said about your future, especially during seasons where you are feeling discouraged or enduring setbacks.

Understand that very often prophecy will bring confirmation, not completely new revelation. That is not to say that God never speaks anything totally fresh through prophetic words. But, most often I have found that a word confirms something I have already had prophesied over me in the past or it reinforces what I am already sensing in my spirit.

If the prophecy is completely 'left-field' or feels 'off', note it down but don't get upset or angry. I remember once at a conference, a young church leader told Becky and me that he had a word for us. While I'm sure he meant well, what he shared was really negative, discouraging, and didn't represent our reality at all. While we did record it at the time, as soon as the young man left, we both immediately decided not to give the word any place in our hearts. Time has proven it to be inaccurate.

Don't jump to conclusions about the interpretation or application. At times, the prophetic word will be direct and require little interpretation. However, very often it will be open to various interpretations and applications. Again, if you have it recorded, you can take the time to pray into it and seek further clarification and understanding.

Don't make major life decisions based on a single prophetic word. Generally, the more important the decision, the greater the level of confirmation required. Dr. Bill Hamon shares the following wise advice:

"Unless God gives us explicit instructions to act upon, the proper response to personal prophecy is simply to continue doing what we have been doing before we received the word of the Lord. This is true even if we have been told of great things we will do in the future."

Even though David was anointed as the next King of Israel, he immediately went back to looking after his father's sheep. The anointing was a prophetic proclamation about his future but there were no specific steps or instructions given at this stage. Over time, God would step-by-step move him closer to his destiny.

Faith and patience are prerequisites. Most prophetic words aren't fulfilled within days or even weeks of being spoken over your life. Sometimes it can be months, years, or even decades before you see them come to pass. God takes as long as it requires to prepare us and to prepare the place He has for us. Therefore, you will need both faith and patience to maintain confidence that God will keep His word.

Hebrews 6: 12 exhorts us to "imitate those who through faith and patience inherit what has been promised."

Faith is also vital because, most of the time, what God speaks to us is so much bigger than our current reality. It seems impossible from our present vantage point. We must believe that if God has truly said it, then nothing is impossible with him.

Don't try to force the word into fulfillment. At times when we receive a prophetic revelation, we consciously or subconsciously begin to change our behavior to try to make it happen.

While we don't want to be passive or nonchalant, nor do we want to force the word to be fulfilled before its time. Simply cooperate with God and when He opens a door, step through it.

Ask God: "Is there any one step I need to take right now that could begin to move me towards my prophetic destiny?" This doesn't mean forcing doors that God isn't opening. It's simply a way to demonstrate your faith and show God that you are taking His word seriously. As Bill Johnson says: "Physical obedience brings spiritual release." When God does something in the spiritual, we need to respond in the physical. When you initiate movement, it creates momentum, and other parts of your life start to align with what God has said.

Also, keep in mind that the one step God shows you may be something that He wants you to give up or leave behind because having it in your life will slow you down or hinder you from making progress. As Hebrews 12: 1 says: "…let us throw off everything that hinders and the sin that so easily entangles. And let us run with perseverance the race marked out for us…"

Pay attention to the signs. If God has given your clear word about your future, doors will open and opportunities will present themselves. Don't miss what God is placing in front of you because you're too preoccupied with other things or because the door He's opening doesn't look exactly how you expected.

Seek the wisdom of others. Proverbs 11: 14 says: "Where there is no counsel, the people fall; But in the multitude of counselors there is safety."

When we receive a word that we aren't sure about, it can be really helpful to share it with other mature Christians that we trust. Ask them: "Does this sound like something God might have for me in the future? Does this align with what you know of me?" Later on, when things get tough or the promise is slow to pass, these same people might encourage you to hold onto what God has spoken.

While this list is by no means comprehensive, I believe the above guidelines will help steward what God speaks to you and over your life.

Let me leave you with some wise words from the respected prophet Dr. Bill Hamon:
"Our personal prophecies may presently be causing us confusion and frustration. They may be discouraging because what was

promised is not happening in the time and way we think it should. They may contradict everything that is now in our life and circumstances. But we must nevertheless wait patiently upon the Lord, and He will fulfill His prophetic word, changing both us and our circumstances. If we press on, privately and patiently pursuing our *rhema* from the Lord, we will eventually possess all our prophetic promises. Every true word from God will come to pass in His predestined purpose and timing."

Practical Exercise: Do you have a book or journal where you record the prophetic words spoken over your life? If not, start one today. Perhaps you have some on your phone, some scribbled in the back of your Bible and some written elsewhere. Pull them all together so you can re-read them prayerfully, asking the Holy Spirit if there is anything you need to do at this time to step closer to the fulfillment of the word of the Lord.

DAY 24

JOURNALING

"Journaling is a strategic tool that has been used throughout the generations as a means of capturing and retaining special moments, special thoughts, special prayers, and special revelations in a personal manner."
(James Goll)

Just recently, I met a friend for lunch. He is also the Worship Pastor of a large, influential church here in Ireland. As I sat down, he slid a piece of paper across the table. "Do you remember that?", he asked. I read the words on the page. It was a prophecy I had given at his church in May 2015. The section he was showing me was a transcription which recorded me as saying: "This church needs to invest in upgrading all of your audio and visual equipment so that you can livestream your services to every city, town and village across this island. You won't need the equipment now, but you will need it in 2020."

I had a vague recollection of saying those words, but as I read them amid the current pandemic where livestreaming has become a necessity for all churches, I was blown away. Imagine that five years ago, God wanted to prepare His people to minister effectively in 2020.

The reason my friend was able to show me this prophecy is because, as a church, they intentionally journal and record every prophetic word they receive. It becomes a part of their prophetic history and allows them to regularly look back and reflect on what God has spoken to them over the 30 years of their existence as a community. They also use it as they prepare to move forward. The voice of God guides their planning and decision making.

Similarly, you can write your own personal prophetic history with God. The most effective way to do this is through journaling.

Throughout this book I have emphasized that prayer is not a monologue; it is a two-way conversation. We talk to the Father and He shares His heart with His children. This might come in the form of Bible verses, thoughts, impressions, pictures, visions, prophetic words, or dreams.

At its most basic level, journaling is simply recording what you say to God and what He says to you. It is writing down your prayers and documenting all the prophetic words you receive from other people as well as any insights and revelation imparted to you as you spend time with the Holy Spirit.

WHY JOURNAL?

In the previous chapter, I explained that prophetic revelation you receive is partial and progressive. **Journaling helps you keep all of the pieces in one place**, so that over time, as they unfold, you can see how they all begin to fit together.

Journaling also helps you become familiar with the Father's voice. (John 10: 4) It can accelerate growth in developing your prophetic gift. This is especially applicable in the early stages of your prophetic journey as you are trying to differentiate God's voice from your own thoughts and imagination. It provides a safe place to practice receiving and processing prophetic revelation without the pressure of public exposure. Over time, you can test what you have heard and written. You will begin to discern a pattern of those prophetic journal entries that have come to pass and understand what made these different from those entries which perhaps weren't from God.

Journaling also helps you remember what the Father has said to you in the past. In the previous chapter, I shared how God had spoken to me as a teenager that one day I would share the Gospel with national leaders. I would never have remembered that prophecy 18 years later if I hadn't recorded it. I can also look at those words that have yet to be fulfilled and continue to expect God to honor His word. When going through challenging times, your old journals can inspire you with faith to keep pressing forward.

Through journaling, you can practice putting what God is saying into a clear and communicable form - a necessary skill for prophecy. Writing it down helps you organize your revelation into a coherent message. Later in this chapter, I will explain how I generally form the prophetic words that I share online. Over time, as I have recorded them, I have learned how to communicate what I believe God is saying with clarity and conciseness.

In his book *The Scribe*, James Goll lists the following five purposes of journaling:

1. To encounter God. This is the primary purpose. Journaling will help you encounter God in a more intimate way. You will hear His voice so you can walk in His ways.
2. To record and retain revelation received from God. If the Father provides living water, you don't want to waste it. Journaling provides a container to capture and keep drinking from the well of life.
3. To aid you in attaining your prayer goals. Journaling helps you to keep track of your prayers and prophetic words. You can look back and see how God has answered your prayers, fulfilled His words, and met your needs in the

past. This will fuel the fire of your prayer life in the present. You can also periodically reflect on prayers and prophetic words that have yet to be fulfilled.
4. To document instructions and guidelines from God. Journaling is a place to record lessons you are learning as you travel along life's journey.
5. To provide a space and place to reflect and evaluate your life. A journal will help you process the events and activities you face and search for the deeper work of God in the midst of your days.

Some people think of journaling as a dry, boring and studious discipline. However, it is actually a diary of personal conversations within a beautiful relationship, tracing the words, whispers and wonders that happen in the secret place.

THREE TYPES OF JOURNALING

(i) Devotional Journaling

This simply records your dialogues with God. It might include what He is showing you as you read and meditate on Scripture, pouring out the desires of your heart, expressing your love and gratitude, recording your prayers, and refining your vision and the goals you have in life.

When I am preparing weekly messages for church, I often sit before the Lord, slowly reading and re-reading the text of Scripture. I write down any thoughts, words, or insights as they come to me. It's amazing how the Holy Spirit will show me things I've never seen before, even with a passage I might have read many times in the past.

For example, just this past week I was preaching on Mark 5 about the woman with the bleeding condition. The story begins with a religious leader called Jairus pleading for Jesus to heal his 12-year-old daughter. The healing is then interrupted by this unnamed woman with this terrible condition that excluded her from civic and religious life. She has suffered like this for 12 years.

As I read it and journaled, I saw some amazing connections that I'd missed in the past. For example, the year the little girl was born was the same year the woman began bleeding. As new life was entering the world, her life started to drain slowly away.

Here was the most exciting revelation though. Jesus not only healed the woman with the bleeding condition, he also called her 'daughter'. This is the only time in the Gospels that Jesus addresses anyone this way. Yes, he was restoring her identity as part of God's family. But maybe there was more than that. Jairus came to Jesus on behalf of his daughter. This woman was all alone. She had no daddy to plead her case. Jesus was stepping into that role and fully accepting her as a daughter, loved and cared for by the Father.

This little revelation was the most impactful part of the entire message. It didn't come through reading commentaries or books by scholars. It came through meditation and journaling.

My own journal also has a list of my dreams, goals, and desires. Some of them are spiritual, many others are very ordinary and practical. I love having one place that I can write down unfiltered what is in my heart and mind.

Our family has moved house numerous times during the past 10 years. It's incredible to open boxes and read old journals, seeing how God has answered so many prayers and fulfilled so many dreams and desires.

(ii) Revelatory Journaling

This is where you record revelatory experiences. The book of Daniel records many of his own revelatory encounters. For example, in Daniel 7: 1 we read:

"In the first year of Belshazzar king of Babylon, Daniel had a dream, and visions passed through his mind as he was lying in bed. He wrote down the substance of his dream."

The entire book of Revelation is a written record of what the Apostle John saw in his visionary experience while on the island of Patmos.

When you receive a prophetic word, vision, dream, or other revelation, immediately write it down. Don't get overly focussed on the interpretation or application. Just record the content.

I journal and record prophetic revelations in various ways. The primary means is simply a little A5 notebook. As I pray, I keep it open, and with a pen in hand, jot down any thoughts, images, ideas, or Bible verses that come to mind.

Almost every prophetic word I receive begins with a single idea or thought. As I pray, I will write down one word or phrase on the page. Often then, as I pray in tongues and ask God for more, I continue to write down other thoughts and ideas around the initial word. If I sense the Holy Spirit stirring something more inside me, I might also start speaking into my phone, allowing the words to flow freely without hindrance or interruption. At the end, I put it all on paper, and form it into a coherent prophetic word. I always ask the Lord for Scriptures to reinforce what I have written.

(iii) Historical Journaling

Much like a simple diary, this is simply documenting the experiences you've had and the lessons you've learned from life's journey. While this may not seem as 'spiritual' as the previous two forms of journaling, you have no idea what impact your records could have on other people at some later stage. For example, when a young girl named Anne Frank recorded what life was like during World War II, I'm sure she had no comprehension that millions of people would be deeply touched by her words for decades to come.

I recently read the published diary of a young couple who moved from Australia to plant a church in the UK 20 years ago. I could relate to so much of their journal as they recounted their struggles, opposition, emotions, and also many highlights and victories. It was one of the most helpful church leadership books I have ever read, even though it was never intended to be such a book. I love reading the raw, real, and authentic experiences of others who are wrestling through some of the same issues as I am facing. I know I'm gaining hard-earned wisdom, not just theoretical ideas and platitudes.

WRITING MATTERS

"I will stand at my watch
and station myself on the ramparts;
I will look to see what he will say to me,
and what answer I am to give to this complaint.

Then the LORD replied:

"Write down the revelation
and make it plain on tablets
so that a herald may run with it.

For the revelation awaits an appointed time;
it speaks of the end
and will not prove false.
Though it linger, wait for it;
it will certainly come
and will not delay."

(Habakkuk 2: 1-3)

In these three verses, we are given some helpful pointers when journaling.

Have a time and place where you wait before the Lord. Habakkuk says that he will "stand" and "station" himself at his watch post. In other words, he will stand still and listen for God to speak. I know that the daily 'quiet time' is no longer as popular as it was 30 years ago when I was born again, but there is simply no substitute for having a daily, disciplined time with God.

Life is too busy and we are too easily distracted to regularly get time with uninterrupted time with God unless it is scheduled. You will know what is the best time for you.

Be expectant that God will speak to you. Habakkuk says, "I will look to see what he will say to me." Believe that God really wants to communicate with you each day. As you wait, you will hear His voice.

Ask God questions and express your thoughts and desires without reserve. Habakkuk says he is waiting for an answer. That implies he has asked God a question. I personally have found it so helpful to write down specific and direct questions to the Lord about many situations. For example, just last week I was dealing with a leadership issue in church. My natural inclination was to jump in and be very direct with some of my team. However, as I asked God what to do, He gave me a totally different strategy which has since proven to be so much more effective.

Write it down. This is really the essence of journaling. Record your communion with God, your dreams and their interpretations, visions, and personal feelings and events that matter to you.

Habakkuk says that we do this so that "a herald may run with it." Often, the herald will be you. As you record what you sense God is saying, over time you begin to see a consistent pattern and perhaps a new direction He is leading you.

Practically, I have found that it is best to keep your journal notes together in one place, such as a notebook, journal, or single folder on your computer. This way, you can refer back to them later.

Also, remember to date all your entries and don't get hung up on correct grammar and spelling when journaling.

Read it again. Habakkuk was told that he should write down what he had received because there would be a period of time before it came about. Therefore, your journal becomes an accurate reminder of revelation God has given you that has not yet come to pass.

Just this past week, I was able to look back at a journal and see how God has fulfilled two different words He spoke to me more than six months ago. It stirs up my faith to hold tightly to those promises and prophecies I have yet to see come to pass.

As you read over your journal at a later stage, you might also come across some things you wrote that, in hindsight, you now realize were not from the Holy Spirit. That's totally okay. Simply erase them. This is not an exercise in perfection but in growth.

Share it with others. When you believe God has spoken to you through journaling, it can be really helpful to ask for input from one or two other mature believers. Obviously, what you share and who you share it with will depend on the content of your writing and the nature of your relationship. But the insights of others can bring increased clarity, interpretation and application to what the Lord has spoken to you.

IT'S ABOUT KNOWING HIM

As we conclude this chapter, let us remember that hearing God's voice is not primarily about knowing information or even receiving revelation; it is about knowing God. We want to grow in our relationship with Him. The focus is always on intimacy with the Father, through the Son, in the presence of the Holy Spirit.

Journaling should lead us to increased worship, deeper devotion, and Godly living.

Practical Exercise: A Prayer asking God to help you hear His voice as you journal:

Father, in the great name of Jesus, I present myself to You. May the Holy Spirit touch me right now with His peace and comfort and wisdom. I want to grow in greater communion with You. I want to be a wise steward of Your revelatory ways, and I want to learn lessons from my life's journey. Therefore, I submit myself to You - Your will and Your word and Your ways. I am asking that You lead me into the right application of journaling that fits into the current season of my life. I want to record the dreams You have for me - big dreams. I need to dream with You, God. I'm excited and looking forward to encountering You through my journaling. Give me the pen of the ready writer as my heart overflows with a good theme, and I address my verses to You, the King above all kings. Amen.

(Adapted from a prayer in *The Scribe* written by James Goll)

DAY 25

THE HEART OF THE PROPHETIC

"Redemptive prophecy is that which speaks to the destiny of God for an individual in a life-bringing, redemptive way."

(Cindy Jacobs)

Once, at the end of a church service where I was the guest preacher, a young man came forward for prayer. He didn't state any specific need, just that he wanted God to meet with him. As I prayed, the Holy Spirit showed me that this man had been involved in homosexual behavior. To be honest, it was a more vivid picture than I would have wanted to receive. So clear, in fact, that I knew the Lord had to be showing me this specific act for a special reason.

I began to declare over him: "God wants to affirm your masculinity. You are a man of God."

The man began to weep and shake.

"You are not what you have done", I continued. "That is not your identity."

Through tears, he began to confess his specific sin to me. I stopped him. "God knows and I know", I told him. "But that is not who you are. You are a man with calling and purpose and destiny."

I then broke off any demonic hold this past behavior had over him and spoke healing and restoration over his body, specifically focusing on those parts the Lord had shown me.

Just over a year later, I was back speaking in the same church. As soon as I walked in, the young man strode across the room, shook my hand, looked me in the eye, and said: "Thank you, Craig. I have never even wanted to back near that sort of life since you prayed for me. I'm free from those desires."

WITHOUT LOVE, IT MEANS NOTHING

Paul primarily writes about prophecy and the gifts of the Holy Spirit in 1 Corinthians 12 and 14. Sandwiched in-between these two exhortations about spiritual gifts is the chapter that you've probably heard read at almost every wedding you've ever attended, 1 Corinthians 13. It's the famous chapter about love.

"If I speak in the tongues of men and of angels, but have not love, I am a noisy gong or a clanging cymbal. And if I have prophetic powers, and understand all mysteries and all knowledge, and if I have all faith, so as to remove mountains, but have not love, I am nothing. If I give away all I have, and if I deliver up my body to be burned, but have not love, I gain nothing.

Love is patient and kind; love does not envy or boast; it is not arrogant or rude. It does not insist on its own way; it is not irritable or resentful; it does not rejoice at wrongdoing, but rejoices with the truth. Love bears all things, believes all things, hopes all things, endures all things.

Love never ends. As for prophecies, they will pass away; as for tongues, they will cease; as for knowledge, it will pass away. For we know in part and we prophesy in part....

...So now faith, hope, and love abide, these three; but the greatest of these is love."

(vv. 1-9; 13)

Paul was being incredibly intentional here in placing an entire chapter devoted to the many aspects of love right in the middle of describing the manifestations of the Holy Spirit. The church at Corinth was somewhat obsessed with the more visible and vocal gifts, so much so that they were misusing them in their services. Paul, however, doesn't prohibit their use. He corrects it, reminding them that if they are used in the absence of real, genuine love for one another, they are nothing more than an annoying noise.

The prophetic gift is never given to draw attention to my spirituality or the other person's sin. It is not a stick to berate or beat the evil out of people. It is an expression of God's heart with the purpose of lifting them up and reminding them of who they are in Christ. That is not to say that you will never have to give a hard or corrective word to someone. That will occasionally happen. But you always move beyond the wrongdoing to speaking God's grace, fresh hope, and the possibility of a new beginning.

Referring to 1 Corinthians 13, well-known prophet Cindy Jacobs says:

"Sometimes I read through this love chapter and repent for any way I have not shown Christlike love. (Maybe I need to do that more than I do. Perhaps we all should.) We need to keep 1 Corinthians 13 in mind as we prophesy to people. If I have a corrective word to give to someone, I will at times walk the floor, praying about it for a couple of days or more, seeking the Lord for the right timing and way to give the word. One of the plumb lines of my prophetic life has to do with my attitude toward the person to whom I am giving a corrective word. If I have any animosity, bitterness or anger in my heart toward the person, or if I relish being the one to give the corrective word because that person has wounded me in any way, I am not the one to give the word. Either I have to cleanse my heart before I give the word or God will use another purer vessel to do His work."

ARE YOU DIGGING FOR DIRT OR TREASURE?

Earlier in this book, I described an event at which I observed a well-known prophet hug a man for a long time bringing deep emotional healing to his wounds of rejection.

Not long after that, I had the opportunity to have lunch with this prophet. I told him how profoundly moved I was by the whole experience. He told me his own story.

Apparently, back in the 1980s and '90s, pastors would bring him in to expose sin in their congregations. He would literally stand at the front and pick out people who were having affairs, stealing from their workplaces, or engaging in other unbiblical behavior. His accuracy was almost 100% and so he felt quite important and smug about how God was using him. Then one day God spoke to him clearer than ever before. God said to him, "If you ever use my gift like that again, I will expose your own sin and remove you from your position of leadership forever." He repented and from that day forward committed that he would use his gift to express the Father's heart.

In Matthew 13, Jesus told a story about treasure hidden in a field. Paul talked about each of us having treasure hidden in jars of clay (2 Cor 4). As we excavate through people's lives, there will always be an opportunity to focus on the dirt and clay. It's not hard to find. I'm sure like me, you're very aware of the sin, failings, and shortcomings in your life. I don't need to be reminded of them. I do, however, need to be told what God has placed inside me, the calling He has on my life, the promises He has spoken over me. The goal of the prophetic is to see past the dirt and uncover the treasure.

As we read through the prophetic books of the Old Testament, even the most severe and harshest judgments were tempered with hope and offers of reconciliation to those who repented. For example, in Jeremiah 15: 19 we read:

"Therefore thus says the LORD:
"If you return, I will restore you,
and you shall stand before me."

Similarly, Ezekiel 33: 1 says:

"Say to them, As I live, declares the Lord GOD, I have no pleasure in the death of the wicked,

but that the wicked turn from his way and live;
turn back, turn back from your evil ways, for why will you die, O house of Israel?"

There will be a day of judgment. The Bible makes that clear. But Jesus paid the price and took God's wrath upon himself at the cross. James 2: 13 says: "Mercy triumphs over judgment." In this age of grace, prophecy never finishes with judgment. There is always some redemptive element that points people to the opportunity to repent, to be restored, and to be reconciled. Mike Bickle says it like this: "We prophesy each time we make known His passionate heart."

Consider the ministry of Jesus. He was constantly being criticized because he spent time with the "sinners" of his day. Didn't he know they were such spiritual reprobates? Of course he did. Yet, he always treated them with value, spoke to them with dignity, and showed them who they could become. He saw who they were created to be and looked at them through a lens of love. His ultimate goal was always to reconnect them with the Father. That's why the woman at the well became an effective evangelist, Zacchaeus willingly returned more money than he had taken, and the thief on the cross ended up in Paradise. They were transformed by love. They were converted by grace. They were moved by mercy.

Shawn Bolz expresses it well:

"The prophetic is one of the greatest tools of love we have…It is the tool that accelerates relationship and creates connection with people, cities, countries, industries, and the world. Through it we see a very real glimpse of God's heart and get to treat people exactly the way God intended them to be treated from the beginning.

…It is supposed to be our way of life - to see people the way God always longed for them to be seen and, from that revelation, to treat them out of his culture of love so that they will want to be the version of themselves we see."

Imagine if we could see and treat one another this way. It would revolutionize our relationships and call us forward into our greatest purpose.

As the father of an eight-year-old boy, I have always been so conscious of the words that I speak over him. He makes many mistakes and sometimes can be hard work. I could point out his faults but that doesn't accomplish much. Instead, I make it my mission to speak over him who he really is, not what he lacks. When he is rude or selfish, I remind him that he is kind and generous, so at that moment, he is acting outside of his true nature.

Even with our church, I tell them every week that they are so generous. Is every member *actually* generous with their finances? No. But as those made in the image of a God whose nature it is to give, generosity is at the core of their spiritual DNA. By calling out of them who they are in Christ, we have experienced a 30% growth in giving every year since I arrived. I love what the late Kim Clement used to say: "I see you in the future and you look much better than you do right now." Prophecy doesn't focus on a single paragraph or a particular chapter of a person's life. It sees them in the context of God's great story of redemption and speaks to them from the perspective of glory.

When we led a church in inner-city Dublin, one especially cold winter a temporary homeless shelter opened just along the street from our building, housing 100 men and women. Many of them were addicts, others were homeless simply because of financial hardship.

We decided that we would make them a Christmas dinner. But this wasn't going to be an ordinary meal. We hired one of the best chefs in the entire city who, along with his team, prepared an amazing five-course meal for our 'guests'. Church members waited on their tables, serving them as if they were royalty. We put on live music. We gave them each a gift card for a local large clothes shop. After they had eaten, we sat with them and listened to their stories. Some of them were truly heartbreaking. We didn't preach. We just cared for them.

At the end of the evening, many of them hugged us with tears running down their faces. That meal didn't solve all of their problems by any stretch. But for one evening they got to experience the love the Father longed to lavish on them.

For most of my life, I have wrestled with insecurity and inferiority. It's only in the past few years that I'm finally starting to feel comfortable in my own skin. I could never have imagined preaching in front of crowds, writing books, and prophesying. Yet, during the past 30 years, men and women have spoken the heart of the Father over my life. They have chosen to see past the dirt and call out the treasure. Rather than focusing on my failures, they have prophesied my potential. Instead of condemning me for my wandering, they have lovingly reminded me of the call of God on my life.

I probably don't know you personally. But I would guess that you're not all that different from me. You have good days and bad days. You struggle in some areas and can't seem to overcome certain weaknesses. At times you feel so confident you could take on the world. Other times you want to pull the duvet over your head and hide from everyone. But deep inside, you know God has created you to make a difference. To make a dent in the world. To be significant. To impact those around you. That's why you're reading this book.

As we look for the treasure among the dirt in other people's lives, let us also look for it in our own lives. Of course, we should seek to live a holy life and repent of sin if we need to. But often we are much harder on ourselves than we are on others. We are experts on the dirt in our lives.

Never forget, under all that dirt is some stunning treasure that God has deposited inside you. If no one else calls it out of you, maybe you should take the initiative and call it out of yourself.

Practical Exercise: Think of a person you really struggle with. Perhaps it's a work colleague, a neighbor, or even a family member. Picture them in your mind. Be honest about their flaws. Admit what it is that you find so difficult about them.

Now ask Jesus to help you see them as he sees them. Say: "Jesus, what do you love about this person?" Keep picturing them. Imagine Jesus is standing in front of them, looking directly into their eyes. Feel the love in his heart. What would he say to them? Write it down. If you're really brave, why not share it with them?

DAY 26

PROPHETIC CHARACTER

"Remember that one of the tests of authenticity is the actual life of the prophet. There is no mandate or excuse for unreasonable, eccentric, or overemotional behavior. We need to act and react in a Christ-like manner and so earn the right to be heard and trusted."

(Rachael Hickson)

As a church leader, I have often had the privilege of hosting well-known, highly-gifted men and women in ministry. From preachers to prophets to healing evangelists to worship leaders, so many of them have been a joy to meet and work alongside. Up close they are more kind, generous, or fun than I could have imagined. I immediately think of John Arnott, formerly the pastor of Toronto Airport Christian Fellowship, the church where the 'Toronto Blessing' broke out in the mid-'90's. When he came to visit, he could not have been more easy-going and humble. He never once mentioned money or an honorarium. That made me want to bless him all the more!

Sadly, there were others (who shall remain unnamed) who were not so pleasant up-close. One well-known healing evangelist, who I had greatly admired from afar, demanded $1000 per day just to be in our country, even when he wasn't ministering. He had already booked a first-class flight to arrive three days before the conference was due to begin. Needless to say, we canceled the event.

When you encounter great gifting without Godly character it leaves a bad taste in your mouth. No matter how anointed the individual is, it's hard to receive their ministry if they're living a life that contradicts Christ-like character and the fruit of the Spirit. That's why it's so vital that, as men and women seeking to grow in our prophetic gifting, we continually seek to deepen our walk with Christ and live a life that honors him in every way. Not that we will be perfect this side of Heaven. But we must be moving towards greater holiness and dealing with those issues in our lives which would undermine our ministry or cause us to stumble.

THE TYPE OF PEOPLE GOD SPEAKS TO

"The secret of the LORD is for those who fear Him,
he makes his covenant known to them."
(Psalm 25: 14)

I don't share my secrets with many people. If I am to open my heart
and disclose my deepest thoughts, I need to know that the other person can be trusted. I believe it's the same with God. He longs to share His heart with His people, but sadly some believers simply don't have the character or maturity to steward what He would tell them.

What are the qualities and characteristics that God looks for in those He wants to speak to?

HUMILITY

"Humility is the pathway to intimacy with God, while arrogance leads to a spiritual desert." (Jack Deere)
Jesus' half-brother once wrote this: "God opposes the proud but gives grace to the humble." (James 4: 6) The Greek word for 'oppose' here literally means that God resists or sets Himself against the proud. It's sobering to think that sometimes, while we are blaming the Devil for blocking our path, it could actually be God resisting us.

However, we should note that the word for grace here is *charis* which can also mean 'favor'. Additionally, it is the root of the word *charismata* which is used for spiritual gifts in the New Testament.

So, taken together, this verse could read: God sets Himself against those who are proud, but he gives favor and imparts gifts to those who are humble.

Pride is something that can creep into our lives very subtly, especially as we grow in giftedness and God increases our visibility or enlarges our platform. I've found this to be especially true in the prophetic. People love to hear what a prophetic person has to say. They appear to have a special hotline to God. Sadly, over time, the prophet can begin to believe the praise and compliments that others lavish upon them. They start to feel entitled to special treatment. They find it difficult to submit to authority or to receive criticism. They are the 'anointed one' after all.

We see this in the life of Saul. In rebuking him, Samuel said: "You were once small in your own eyes..." (1 Sam 15: 17) As Saul had grown in stature and status, he had moved from genuine humility to a place of pride, entitlement and disobedience. Ultimately the Lord removed His anointing because Saul had disqualified himself from leadership.

It's so important to remember that spiritual gifts are just that – gifts. You didn't earn them, nor do you deserve them. They are not a trophy to be shown off, they are a tool to be used to equip the church and serve others. As Jack Deere says: "Humility and the ability to hear God's voice go hand in hand. Every person in the Bible who had a great ability to hear God's voice was also a person of great humility."

AVAILABILITY

Hearing the voice of God with clarity and consistency requires that you are willing to lay down your life in submission and surrender to the Father. There is no shortcut or substitute. Even Jesus, throughout his ministry, made it a regular practice to get away from the crowds so he could be with the Father (Mk 1: 35; Luke 4: 42; 5; 15). As you look at the life of Jesus, he was never hurried, stressed, or flustered. Even though the demands upon him were great, he was never in a rush. This is because he looked upon his time as his Father's time. He was completely available for whatever the Father planned for him each day. He only did what he say his Father doing (John 5: 19). He was always in the right place at the right time to fulfill the will of the Father.

What I am talking about here is more than having a daily 30 minute daily 'quiet time' with God, as helpful as that can be. It is about offering your every minute of your day to God at home, in the workplace, as you shop for groceries, and as you engage in your hobbies. It is being attentive to the whisper of the Spirit in the midst of chaos and noise all around. It is experiencing His presence and listing for His voice throughout the day in all situations.

As a pastor, I used to believe I had to be available to everyone, all the time. I was pulled in so many different directions and was worn out. Now I am much more focused and intentional in how I spend my time. I seek to discern what the Father is already doing and partner with Him. I listen for His voice as I interact with church members and visitors. I feel free to say 'no' rather than to continually overschedule myself in attempting to please people. I get as much done, if not more, but without the stress and anxiety.

This also affects my prayer life. I spend time with God every day, normally first thing. However, once or twice a week he may wake me up in the early hours of the morning (around 4.00 am). I simply climb out of bed, go into my study, get on my knees, and remain there until I believe He has finished speaking. Those are often the times when I hear Him with the greatest clarity. It's almost as if the Father has decided: "If he will make time for me, I'll make it worth his while."

When Jesus chose his twelve apostles, we read that, above all else, they were selected "that they might be with him and he might send them out to preach and have authority to cast out demons." (Mark 3: 14-15) Presence with Jesus came before power for preaching and ministry. Fruitfulness flows from intimacy which can only happen when there is availability.

OBEDIENCE

"God speaks to those who are willing to do whatever He says to them." (Jack Deere)

As a pastor, people often ask me for advice about certain issues or dilemmas they are facing. Over time, however, what I have realized is that they aren't really looking for my input or wisdom. They simply want me to affirm what they have already decided in their hearts to do. Anyone who has ever served in youth ministry will know exactly what I'm talking about. A teenage Christian girl comes along and needs advice about a boy she wants to date. She tells you that he's not a believer but he's not against Christianity. Plus, she might be able to bring him to Christ. You express your opinion that it's not a good idea. That, if she's going to date at all, it should be with a committed Christian. She thanks you for your advice and a week later you see her walking hand in hand through the mall with the non-Christian guy.

Imagine this happened a number of times. At some point, you would simply tell her: "I'm not going to tell you what I think because it doesn't change how you live."

Often we ask for God to speak to us, yet when He does, we don't obey because we don't like what He is telling us. It's inconvenient or involves sacrifices that we'd prefer not to make. We don't outright tell Him 'no'. We simply get on with our lives as if he'd never spoken. If this continues, at some point, God will go silent. Why would He waste His words on those who don't want to hear them?

The reason Jesus heard the Father's voice better than anyone was his total desire to be obedient, no matter what the cost. He said, "By myself I can do nothing; I judge only as I hear, and my judgment is just, *for I seek not to please myself but him who sent me*" (John 5: 30). When God sees that willingness in our hearts, He will speak to us freely and frequently.

As a family, we have determined that we will go wherever God tells us. No matter how settled or comfortable we are, how much we love our house, or how much our son enjoys his friends, if God speaks, we move. Because of that, when He does speak, it is clear and unmistakable. Every place He has sent us has been difficult in different ways, but I can honestly say that because of our obedience, we have experienced an inordinate amount of favor and blessing on our lives and ministry.

In John 14: 23 we read:

"Jesus replied, "Anyone who loves me will obey my teaching. My Father will love them, and we will come to them and make our home with them."

Obedience and intimacy with God go hand-in-hand. If you want to hear God, do what He says.

PURITY

"Our responsibility is to always be a clean and consecrated vessel through which the Holy Spirit can minister." (Helen Calder)

"Above all else, guard your heart, for everything you do flows from it." (Proverbs 4:23)

Even the cleanest water, if it flows through an unclean conduit, becomes tainted. In seeking to hear and communicate the voice of God, we must seek to live lives of holiness and purity. Again, I am not saying that if you sin you are disqualified from prophetic ministry. I would have been ruled out long ago. What I am saying is that being clean and being close to God go together. Jesus himself said, "Blessed are the pure in heart, for they will see God." (Matt 5: 8) If we are to seek intimacy with the Father, we need to deal with those areas of our lives where there might be blockages to His blessing. These could include lust, pornography, bitterness, unforgiveness, pride, greed, jealousy, anger, negativity, etc.

In the Old Testament, the word of the Lord was spoken verbatim through the prophets. For example, in Jeremiah 1: 9 we read, Then the LORD put forth His hand and touched my mouth, and the LORD said to me "Behold I have put My words in your mouth." That is why they could literally say, "Thus saith the Lord."

Today, much more often, prophecy is expressed through His people in a less clear and defined way. It gets filtered through our personalities, prejudices and past. Jesus himself said, "For out of the overflow of the heart, the mouth speaks." (Luke 6: 45)

If we have unrepentant sin and unresolved issues, these will likely distort, corrupt, or pollute what we are sharing. As John the Baptist said concerning himself and Jesus, "He must increase, but I must decrease." (John 3: 30)

COURAGE

"Prophets are fundamentally warriors, who know how to set captives free with words that liberate and fight on the recipient's behalf." (Emma Stark)

Prophets need to say what God tells them to say, even if it's not popular, 'cool', or politically correct. They are not seeking the approval of men but rather live for an audience of One. God commissioned Jeremiah with these words: "You must go to everyone I send you to and say whatever I command you. Do not be afraid of them…" (1: 7-8)

Courage is especially needed in today's Western 'cancel' culture where there is so much pressure to conform to societal norms, especially around politics, sexuality, and moral issues. John the Baptist literally lost his head because he refused to capitulate to the powers and stay silent about the immorality he had witnessed (see Mark 6).

This, of course, does not mean a prophetic person should intentionally be rude or offensive. Nor does the prophet have to be a constant negative herald of doom and gloom. On occasions, prophecy will confront the prevailing culture and call for repentance. At other times it will be incredibly affirming and encouraging.

Don't assume that someone who rails against liberal morality or politics is prophetic. Maybe they just have unresolved anger issues. Jesus always spoke the truth with directness and great authority but never with disrespect or arrogance. Yes, he overturned the tables in the temple and conflicted with the religious leaders. But he also detracted attention away from the woman caught in adultery who was about to be stoned and spent time with "tax collectors and sinners".

Humility, purity, obedience, and courage all flow together in the prophetic person's life to bring a beautiful balance of Christ-like authority and integrity. When they speak, people listen, not because of the volume of their tone, but because of the anointing on their life.

All Christians represent God here on earth. We are Christ's ambassadors (2 Cor 5: 20). Through us, he reveals himself to the world. Therefore, our lives and lifestyle matter. Our character and conduct will either support what we proclaim or negate it. You can be incredibly gifted and prophetically accurate, yet if you are proud, rude, or negative, you will do more harm than good. Therefore it is vital to walk closely with Christ, submit to Godly authority, and deal with any issues in your life that will hinder you from walking in the fullness of life Jesus died to give you.

Practical Exercise: Which of the above five character traits – humility, availability, obedience, purity, courage - do you struggle with most?

If it is lust or obedience, is there someone who you can pray with and who can keep you accountable?

If there are any unresolved issues that you need to deal with, such as bitterness or unforgiveness, what can you do **today** to remove these hindrances and move forward?

DAY 27

PROPHETIC EVANGELISM

"Today, people are hungry for an authentic Christianity, evidenced by the power of God, and walked out in daily living. Whether it's the boardroom, the back room, or the back alley, a fitting word from Heaven, at the appropriate time, delivered in love, sets people free from their mistaken notions of Christianity. It introduces them to a consuming and fulfilling relationship."
(Tommy Barnett)

I sat at the hospital bedside of Tom, a man in his late-40's who was clearly dying. I had never met him before, but some relatives who attended our church had asked me to visit. The doctors had advised Tom's wife that the cancer was so advanced he only had one or two weeks left. We chatted about his life, the two little Russian boys he and his wife had recently adopted, and his faith. Like many in Ireland, Tom was a traditional Catholic but rarely attended church.

As we talked, the Holy Spirit was whispering the word 'trauma'. Eventually, when he stopped to take a sip of water, I asked Tom, "Have you had experienced any significant trauma in the past seven years?"

He paused for a second and then told me about a serious car accident that had happened around five years before.

The Holy Spirit whispered again, "That's not it."

I gently pressed further, "No, that's not it, was there something else?"

He looked somewhat surprised, but then slowly began to open up about an incident that had happened seven years before.

Tom had been a school teacher and was accused of abusing one of the children in his class. He was immediately suspended from his job and it didn't take long before the local community started to label him as a pedophile.

Eventually, the 'victim' confessed that they had made the entire story up. It was a complete fabrication. Tom was reinstated to his job and, as I said, was even permitted to adopt two children.

However, he lived with a constant cloud of suspicion over his life. He was completely consumed with anger that one false accusation had ruined his life. This had led to a significant stronghold of offense, bitterness and unforgiveness developing in his heart.

As I shared the Gospel and spoke with Tom about the saving work of Jesus, he broke down, weeping loudly. I told him he needed forgiveness for his sins, but that he also needed to forgive his accuser. It took a while, but eventually he chose to let go of his anger and leave it up to God to vindicate him.

Along with his wife, Tom prayed. They both opened their hearts to receive Christ as Lord and Savior. A supernatural peace flooded the little hospital room. The presence of the Lord was tangible. We could all feel it. When I looked at Tom, his entire countenance had been transformed. His wife could see it too. He radiated joy and peace.

I would love to tell you that Tom was physically healed. Sadly, that wasn't the case. He died a few weeks later. But he died a 'good death', surrounded by those he loved, free from anger, totally confident that he was going to be with Jesus.

In the month that followed, many of Tom's relatives started coming to our church, every one of them finding new life in Christ.

NOT EVANGELISM!

Let's begin with the honest admission that the word 'evangelism' is enough to put most Christians off even reading this chapter. (That is unless you are an evangelist.) The thought of sharing our faith with strangers, never mind friends, causes most of us to instinctively shrink back and leave it to the 'experts' or to resign ourselves to hoping that non-Christians will see virtuous qualities in our lives and somehow be drawn to Christ. After all, didn't Jesus say, "Preach the Gospel at all times, and if necessary, use words"? No, Jesus did not say that. He was too busy preaching and demonstrating the Gospel of the Kingdom! (The quote is attributed to Saint Francis of Assisi and even then, there is actually no historical or literary evidence that he ever said such words.)

It is true, of course, that our entire lives should point to the reality of the Gospel. However, if we are to take seriously the command of Jesus to "Go into all the world and preach the gospel to all creation" (Mark 16: 15), we must understand that this will involve words as well as actions. As Paul said in Romans 10: 14:

"How, then, can they call on the one they have not believed in? And how can they believe in the one of whom they have not heard? And how can they hear without someone preaching to them?"

The Father has only given one group of people the responsibility to share His love to a lost and broken world – the church. That includes you and me. If we don't do it, they simply won't hear. And if they don't hear, not only will they miss out on a relationship with their Creator, they will also spend eternity separated from God. We have a mission and a mandate from Heaven that we dare not ignore.

PROPHECY FOR UNBELIEVERS?

Prophetic evangelism can be defined simply as God using revelatory phenomena to speak to the hearts of those who don't know Jesus. For too long, the prophetic has been confined to within the four walls of the church. We have seen it as a tool primarily to strengthen and encourage believers. However, in recent years some believers have dared to believe that the Holy Spirit also wants to speak to lost people, waking them up to the reality that Jesus is alive and knows them personally. The conclusion has largely been that, when prophecy is combined with evangelism, the results are exponential. Hearts are unlocked and people who were far from God come home to the Father.

We shouldn't be surprised that God would speak to unbelievers. In the Old Testament, prophecy was used to bring pagan people to a knowledge of Yahweh. Joseph employed 'dream interpretation in his witness to Pharaoh. Elijah and Elisha both used prophecy to in their witness to pagans. And Daniel was used powerfully to share revelation with Nebuchadnezzar, the king of Babylon.

As we enter the New Testament, apart from the ministry of Jesus which we will look at shortly, Peter used prophecy on the day of Pentecost to convince the crowd that what they were witnessing had been foretold by the prophets. As we continue through the book of Acts, the Spirit speaks and hearts are opened.

A THIRST SATISFIED

Jesus' entire ministry was based upon listening to the Father and responding. In John 5: 19 he said, "I tell you the truth, the Son can do nothing by himself; he can do only what he sees his Father doing, because whatever the Father does the Son also does."

We see a powerful example of this in John 4. Jesus is returning from Judea to Galilee. He finds himself compelled to go through Samaria where, at midday, he stops at Jacob's well for a drink.

Just then a woman approaches carrying a heavy stone water jar. She is shocked when Jesus asks her for a drink. She can tell from his appearance that he is a Jew. As a woman and a Samaritan, Jesus should not have even been speaking to her. She points out that Jesus is breaking the rules. Jesus pivots the conversation and begins to talk about "living water" that can truly quench one's thirst.

The woman is intrigued. She says that she would like this "living water" so she doesn't have to keep returning to the well day after day.

At this point, Jesus receives revelation from the Father and decides to press further. "God and fetch your husband," he tells her.

"I don't have a husband," the woman replies.

And now we have the key moment where Jesus shares an insight into her life – an insight not learned by human means but through prophetic revelation.

He says, "That's true. You don't have a husband. You've been married five times and the man you're currently living with isn't your husband."

There is a stunned silence. The woman is wondering how this complete stranger could know so much about her. Then she sees it. He is a prophet.

She begins to talk about religion. Jesus points her away from human traditions to himself. He tells her that he is the long-awaited Messiah.

The woman drops her water jar and runs back to her town. A curious crowd gathers, following her back towards Jesus. John concludes the story by telling us, "Many of the Samaritans from that town believed in him because of the woman's testimony." (John 4: 39)

As a result of one prophetic revelation, a spiritual harvest occurred in the most unlikely of places. An insight from the Father unlocked her heart and transformed this Samaritan woman into a soul winner.

Today, more than ever, like this woman, people need a personal encounter with the God who loves them. The lost are stumbling around in the dark, desperate for a sense of meaning and purpose. They will drink from any source that offers temporary satisfaction or relief. Often, instead of consuming refreshing water, they ingest polluted filth that only leaves them feeling more empty and thirsty than before.

As the church, our calling has never changed. We are the representatives of Jesus to a broken world, calling to proclaim and demonstrate the Gospel of the Kingdom. We do this through preaching, prophesying and practical compassion. Even the most hardened and stubborn heart can be unlocked with a revelation or insight that can only have come from a non-natural source.

EVERYONE, EVERYDAY, EVERYWHERE

Imagine walking into your local coffee shop. You know the barista by name but you've never had a proper conversation. As you're standing in line, the Holy Spirit whispers to you that her dad has just been diagnosed with a terminal illness. As you're ordering, you ask if she's okay. She says she's fine. You gently ask if everything is alright with her family. Her eyes fill with tears. You say, "God wants you to know that He loves you and He loves your dad. I'm going to be praying for your dad that he is healed." She thanks you and you pay for your coffee. Over the next few months, you continue to converse with her and pray. However things turn out, do you think that she might be more open to coming to church or an event than she would have been before? Most likely, yes.

For too long evangelism has been left to the 'experts'. We don't feel equipped or knowledgeable enough, so we rely on evangelists and missionaries to do the work that we are all called to. Sadly, much church growth today is not through conversions. Rather, it is largely due to believers moving from one place of worship to another. That was never God's intention. His desire is that every empowered believer shares their faith in naturally supernatural ways, every day, in every place. It doesn't have to be that difficult.

Jesus once told His disciples to let down their nets for a catch of fish. They had worked hard all night for nothing, but when they let down the net at Jesus' word, a miracle happened. The net was filled to overflowing with fish. (Luke 5: 4-6)

This is a great illustration of prophetic evangelism. When we partner with the Holy Spirit, miracles happen. Prophetic evangelists don't rely on their abilities to persuade people; they rely on the Holy Spirit's ability to reveal. Our job is to share Christ and to follow the finger of God. If I do what God wants me to do, He'll bring the fruit.

In every part of your neighborhood - the office, the gym, the park, the supermarket – there are people who need Jesus. Most of them just don't realize it yet. What they do know is that there has to be more to this life than they are currently experiencing. They are longing for meaning and purpose, freedom from shame and guilt, a way out of addiction, a community where they can belong, a sense of self-worth and acceptance. Christ offers all of this and so much more.

So, what can you do?

First, make sharing the Gospel a priority. We must get over our apathy or reluctance to share our faith with unbelievers.

Evangelism (or whatever you want to call it) is not an optional extra in the Christian life. It is absolutely central and core to what it means to be a Jesus-follower. Understand just how much lost people matter to God. Remind yourself what your own life would be like if you didn't know Christ. Ask God to stir up your heart again with a passion for the lost.

Second, ask God for more prophetic insight. As you go about your day, be constantly conversing with the Father. In each place and space you enter, ask Him, "Is there anyone you want to speak to here?" I have discovered that people who have never prophesied in church will receive clear and detailed words for the unchurched. All it takes is a willingness to ask and the courage to share.

Third, be ready. As you go about your day, be attentive and open to what is going on around you. Take out the earphones and actually have conversations with people. Stop rushing away. Look at them, listen to them, show that you care. Be prepared to be interrupted or inconvenienced.

Fourth, be obedient to whatever God tells you. At times the Holy Spirit may ask you to do or say something that makes no sense. For example, a friend of mine once walked into Starbucks and saw a young woman sitting alone. My friend sensed the Holy Spirit say, "Go and show her your scars." Before receiving Christ, for years she had self-harmed. Consequently her arms and legs were covered in scars. She kept them covered as much as possible, so she recoiled at the thought of showing them to a complete stranger. Yet, the Lord kept speaking clearly, "Go over and show her your scars." Eventually she got up from her table and walked slowly across to where the young lady was sitting. She introduced herself and said something along the lines of, "You're probably going to think I'm crazy. Sometimes I think I hear God speak to me and just there I sensed him telling me to show you my scars." She pulled up her sleeve as she spoke. The young lady starting crying. She pulled up her sleeves and both her arms were covered in scars. Her legs were also marked. They talked for a while, exchanged details, and a few weeks later the young lady went to church with her new friend. Not only did she encounter Jesus, but a month later someone prayed for her and her scars almost totally disappeared. I actually have photos of her lower legs 'before' and 'after' she received prayer. The difference is incredible.

Finally, don't let the enemy stop you. There will be days when you will get it wrong. Or the other person may not react well. Satan hates it when God's people operate in our full authority, so he will constantly tell you how unqualified or useless you are. I find it helpful to remember that I am more fearful about giving a work than an unbeliever is likely to be about receiving one. Do not let the enemy immobilize you through lies and fear. Resist him and get back out there.

My friend Mark Marx has developed an incredible ministry called Healing on the Streets (HOTS) which is now being used in almost every city across the globe. It's pretty simple. A huge banner with 'HEALING' printed on it is placed beside empty chairs and passers-by are encouraged to stop for prayer. If you've never been involved in ministry like this, you will be stunned at just how open people are to receiving prayer. Those ministering kneel on the ground in front of them as a sign of humility and service. Often, as the person receives prayer, God will begin to speak about other areas of their life. HOTS is a powerful tool for taking prophetic evangelism into our cities and towns in a proven and non-threatening way.

Jesus said, in John 4:35, "The harvest is ripe." I believe that to be true today. People now are more open to know about Jesus than ever before. Although I believe in all different types of evangelism, prophetic evangelism is so powerful because it cuts through the deception of sin and reveals a supernatural, personal God.

Practical Exercise: In the next 24 hours, ask God to show you one piece of information about someone as you go about your day. It doesn't have to be a complete stranger, just someone you don't know very well.

Expect it to be really simple. God might show you that they have a black dog or that they have applied for a new job.

You might test the word by asking something like, "My son keeps asking me for a dog. Do you have one?" Or, "Do you like working here? What else would you like to do?"

DAY 28

HOW TO SPOT A FALSE PROPHET

"Why can't otherwise God-loving, wonderful people see through the lies of a false prophet? One reason is that false prophets genuinely can be charismatic, fun, entertaining, and even spiritually gifted. They just aren't plugged into the right source." **(Shawn Bolz)**

We decided to visit a local church on our family vacation a few years ago. We entered the hotel conference room where the meeting was taking place and took our seats just as the service was beginning. The pastor welcomed everyone and enthusiastically informed us that we were blessed to have Prophet David with us that day. Following the worship and a short message from the pastor, Prophet David was handed the microphone. To say that what transpired over the next 30-40 minutes was bizarre would be an understatement. With his right leg constantly shaking violently, the 'prophet' called individuals and couples up to the front and uttered the weirdest 'prophet words' over them. Things like, "I see a horse crossing a tightrope, playing a guitar. Does that mean anything to you?" At the end of each word, he would blow on their faces, expecting them to fall over. No one did. I know it's wrong, but I stayed on to watch from a sense of amusement as much as anything else. In the end, we'd all had enough. We got up and walked out.

This guy was definitely strange but also probably quite harmless. It was clear to anyone with an ounce of wisdom that he wasn't a genuine prophet. I can't imagine he got too many speaking invitations and was probably only permitted to share in this gathering because he was a friend of the pastor.

However, not all false prophets are so easy to recognize. Some are much more subtle and sophisticated in their methods. They may be extremely charismatic and convincing figures. Others even think they are operating as genuine prophets but are simply misguided.

As I was writing this chapter, Jeremiah Johnson posted on social media about 'Five Types of Dysfunctional Prophets'.

Seagull Prophets: these are people who in the name of 'prophetic ministry' fly into churches, make a bunch of noise, spew on everyone, and then fly out as quickly as they flew in. It leaves a really bad taste in the mouth of leaders and saints.

Parking Lot Prophets: these are people who corner you when no one else is around and say odd and strange things without having to be held accountable for anything they have said. They typically prophesy things that your church leaders and close friends would take issue with. They leave you confused and even rejecting the prophetic altogether.

Wallet Prophets: these are people who use manipulation in their prophecies to take advantage of your pockets through flattery and distortion. They typically guarantee impossible circumstances will come to pass quickly. they constantly talk about sowing seed, cashapps, and material possessions.

Bleeding Prophets: these are people who have serious emotional wounding and it bleeds through in their prophetic words. Although some of what they say seems to be from the Lord, the other half is in question and leaves you confused. They have been to way too many churches and rejected by every leader you can think of.

Who's Who Prophets: these are people who will preface what they have to say by telling you how anointed they are, how long they have prophesied, and what prophet they have sat under, or whose prophetic school they have attended. Their latest photoshoot and flyer are way more anointed than they actually are in person.

I have to say that while I find all of the above observations amusing, they are also sadly true.

WHAT IS A FALSE PROPHET?

The great challenge for the church is to properly discern those who are genuine from those who are false. The Bible warns us of a great increase in deception, specifically mentioning a great increase of false prophets within the Church (see 1 John 4:1-6, Matthew 7:15, 2 Peter 2:1, 2 Corinthians 11:13-15). Jesus taught that "false prophets will arise and perform great signs and wonders, so as to lead astray, if possible, even the elect." (Matthew 24:24) Today, all over the world we are seeing people rising up and calling themselves prophets of God, so it is vital that we properly weed out the false from the true.

The prevalence of false prophets is not a new issue for God's people. Throughout Scripture they appear in various guises and are deemed as being 'false' for different reasons. From my own study, I have identified three main categories of false prophets in the Bible.

1. Prophets who operate using a spirit of divination.

Divination is defined as "the practice of seeking knowledge of the future or the unknown by supernatural means." In one sense, this should be the most obvious type of false prophet. Yet, they can also be the most deceptive. They may appear to have genuine supernatural power and knowledge, but it comes from a source other than the Holy Spirit.

In Deuteronomy 18: 10-12 we read:

"Let no one be found among you who sacrifices their son or daughter in the fire, who practises divination or sorcery, interprets omens, engages in witchcraft, or casts spells, or who is a medium or spiritist or who consults the dead. Anyone who does these things is detestable to the LORD…"

The pagan nations surrounding Israel regularly consulted mediums and spiritists in the hopes of attaining insight into the future and achieving personal gain. Yahweh commanded that His people live only by His Word and trust Him for the future.

Later, in 1 Samuel 28, King Saul, at perhaps the lowest point of his rule, disguised himself and went to visit the medium, the witch of Endor. He asks the medium to call up Samuel from the dead. Samuel appears, and confronts Saul, predicting that he's going to die in battle. In his next confrontation with the Philistines, Samuel's words come to pass.

The point of the chapter is not that divination or the work of mediums is impossible, but that it is to be avoided at all costs by God's people because it is an assault on God's wisdom, authority and love, and is therefore in the category of idolatry, rebellion and abomination.

In the New Testament, in Acts 16, the Apostle Paul was in Philippi. We read:

"As we were going to the place of prayer, we were met by a slave girl who had a spirit of divination and brought her owners much gain by fortune-telling. She followed Paul and us, crying out, "These men are servants of the Most High God, who proclaim to you the way of salvation." And this she kept doing for many days. Paul, having become greatly annoyed, turned and said to the spirit, "I command you in the name of Jesus Christ to come out of her." And it came out that very hour." (vv. 16-18)

Was this girl speaking the truth? Yes. Was she saying anything against God or Paul? No. But the spirit from which she attained her information was not the Holy Spirit so Paul banished it.

Today, especially in certain parts of the world, the spirit of divination is alive and well, even within the church. Self-styled prophets and apostles may demonstrate miraculous powers and have supernatural insight, but it is counterfeit power that has only been attained through agreement with demonic spirits. In her recent book *Discerning Prophetic Witchcraft*, author Jennifer LeClaire warns:

"The deception about which Jesus and New Testament writers warned is happening now on a large scale. It's not only emanating from prophetic merchandisers on late-night Christian TV with money gimmicks and miracle products we quite easily recognize as a scam. This deception is more subtle in the 21st century....

.... Some conference hosts are inviting people in to speak because they are enamored with a gift, not knowing until it's too late - or perhaps never knowing - that they are helping a false prophet propagate witchcraft. Some conference hosts find out after it's too late and have to make tough decisions. Many make the wrong ones and, at best, are complicit in releasing a spirit of error over those who come to their conferences. At worst, their attendees walk away with empty pockets, false prophetic promises, and demonic impartations."

As a church leader, I have learned the hard way to be incredibly careful about who I invite to minister to our congregation. Nowadays, unless I know them personally or they come recommended by someone whom I trust, they simply won't be permitted to speak. The congregation I serve has confidence that I will never expose them to false teaching.

2. Prophets who speak their own words, not God's.

There have always been individuals of influence within the community of faith who will only 'prophesy' what the majority want to hear. Rather than proclaim the 'word of the Lord', they manufacture words that appeal to the desires of the listener. God spoke through Jeremiah about such people:

"This is what the LORD Almighty says:

'Do not listen to what the prophets are prophesying to you;
they fill you with false hopes.
They speak visions from their own minds,
not from the mouth of the LORD." (Jeremiah 23: 16)

These 'prophets' concocted supposed revelations for the purpose of popularity among the people and also to offer a false sense of security. They spoke of blessing, peace and prosperity, even when the Lord was clearly displeased with His people.

We see the same thing in Ezekiel 13: 1-2:

"The word of the LORD came to me:

'Son of man, prophesy against the prophets of Israel who are now prophesying. Say to those who prophesy out of their own imagination: "Hear the word of the LORD!"

These prophets were actually declaring, "Hear the word of the Lord" and then speaking lies and falsehoods. They were making it all up. It was fiction designed to placate the crowds or elevate the stature of the prophet.

As someone who seeks to share prophetic encouragement online, there is a huge temptation to post more often or to only post things that I know everyone will like. We (almost) all want to be popular and for our social media accounts to grow. Posting a positive word every day is a sure way to attract more followers.

That is not to say that genuine words must be negative. Not at all! The Lord does want to encourage His people and speak hope into their lives. But there are also times when He does ask me to share something more direct, challenging, or seemingly 'negative'. Such was the case with my word for 2020. These 'words' never get as many likes and often lead to people unsubscribing from my email list. However, I genuinely try to only share what I sense the Lord saying.

Also, there are times when I won't post a fresh word for weeks or even months. I then receive concerned messages asking if I'm okay. The truth is, sometimes I don't hear God's voice as clearly as at other times. I go through dry seasons when Heaven seems silent. Then, the wilderness will end and I'll start to share much more frequently again.

Political correctness and people pleasing with ultimately destroy the effectiveness of any prophet or preacher.

3. Prophets who use their gift for personal gain.

These signs of a false prophet can overlap at times. For example, someone with a spirit of divination can make a lot of money through accurately foretelling the future, as can a prophet who draws a crowd by only telling people what they want to hear. However, the primary motivation is typically different. The one who speaks from a spirit of divination is seeking power. The one who tickles people's ears with positive words is seeking popularity. And the one who uses the gift for their own gain is seeking prosperity.

We see this in the case of Balaam in Numbers 20-22. When tempted to use his authentic prophetic gift to obtain riches and glory for himself at the expense of God's people, he eventually gave in.

If you scan through the lists of popular shows and movies on Netflix you will see that people are generally fascinated with all things supernatural. Increasingly, within the church, prophets can garner much attention and even adulation. An evangelism or missions conference will often struggle to attract attendees but a prophetic conference with a 'big name' minister is almost guaranteed to draw a crowd. A prophet with a proven track record of accuracy can gain a huge following as people long to receive a word of direction for their own lives or even an 'impartation' to operate under the same anointing as the prophet. The temptation to minister for material gain must be huge. Sadly, some have succumbed and actually charge people a minimum of $50 for personal prophetic words online.

In his book *Cleansing and Igniting the Prophetic*, Jeremiah Johnson laments:

"I see a trend rising in the Church in which prophets are acting like and even being treated as magicians, prostitutes, and pimps. On stages and throughout the Internet, many offer their prophetic services to anyone who can fill their pockets with money, promote their ministry, and fuel book sales. These men and women are acting like modern-day prophetic whores. They find stimulation through stroking the ego and flesh of leaders and people, all at the expense of the purity and fresh anointing that we so desperately need in the prophetic movement."

Strong words indeed. But sadly, in some cases, they are true. I regularly receive messages offering money in return for personal prophetic ministry online. I always refuse. Yes, I sell books that I have invested hundreds of hours into writing. And I often receive an honorarium when I speak at a church or conference. But, I believe, to charge people for personal prophecy would be to prostitute a spiritual gift and bring dishonor to the Lord.

HOW TO SPOT A GENUINE PROPHET

We have devoted much time in this chapter to highlighting the characteristics and practises of false prophets. However, one of the best ways to recognize the counterfeit is to become familiar with the authentic.

Here are some marks of Biblical, prophetic ministry:

Good Fruit: What is the overall outcome of their ministry? Does it lead to Godly living and a passion for Christ?

Does their character demonstrate the fruit of the Holy Spirit?

Jesus said, "Watch out for false prophets. They come to you in sheep's clothing, but inwardly they are ferocious wolves. By their fruit you will recognize them." (Matthew 7: 15-16)

Any ministry that promotes greed, immorality, or division is not functioning under the power of the Holy Spirit.

Proven Track Record: This relates to the accuracy of the prophetic words they have given in the past but also their reputation over time.

If a 'prophet' consistently gives false predictions about the future, there's a very good chance that they are more interested in fame and sensationalism than in promoting the message of Christ. That is not to say that even the most anointed prophets don't get it wrong at times. But there should be an overall high level of accuracy if they are to be recognized as a prophet.

Also, they should have a good reputation among leaders widely within the Body of Christ. While I believe restoration to the ministry of those who fall into sin is possible, in some charismatic circles we have become much too quick at glossing over blatant immorality and placing 'ministers' back into the pulpit.

Scripturally Sound: It should go without saying that the utterances from a genuine prophet will never contradict the written Word of God. Nor will they constantly take Scriptures out of context.

Now, I understand that not every prophesy can necessarily be backed up by a multitude of Bible verses. For example, if a prophet were to tell you that the Lord is going to open up a new door for ministry to the poor in your community, it would be difficult to give chapter and verse to support that. Yet, overall, as you read through the Bible, you would know that God loves the poor and longs that His people show compassion to them.

Christ-Centred: Genuine prophets not only keep the focus on the person and work of Jesus in their words, but they express the heart of Jesus through their actions and even the tone with which they prophesy. Some well-known leaders today in the Body of Christ seem to believe that prophecy is only genuine if it renounces sin and calls down judgment. Is that what Jesus did? I accept that Jesus did confront unrighteousness, especially among the so-called 'religious'. But when it came to the 'tax collectors and sinners' in society, he demonstrated compassion and mercy.

Accountable: A genuine prophet will be part of a local body of believers and be accountable to overseers. Frankly, I have little time for the itinerant 'man of God' who believes he is only answerable to the Lord. They are generally arrogant and refuse to be under authority because they know their lifestyle would be challenged if it were to come under Godly scrutiny. A true prophet will demonstrate humility, listen to advice and correction, and will submit fully to the leadership in whatever church they are ministering.

While this list is by no means comprehensive, it does provide a helpful way for you to distinguish genuine prophetic ministry from that which is false.

In the coming days, I believe we will see a proliferation of false prophets. Sadly, many believers are so Biblically illiterate that they are willing to believe anything that is 'prophesied' if it is packaged right or appeals to their own personal desires. We will need discernment, a knowledge of God's Word, and a dependence on the Holy Spirit to navigate through the perilous times that lie before us.

Practical Exercise: This is an ongoing exercise. The next time you listen to prophetic people in-person and online, ask yourself:
Do they represent Jesus well?
Are they Scripturally sound?
Do they have a track record of accuracy and a longstanding reputation for Godly character?
Do you discern the Holy Spirit working in their ministry?

DAY 29

STIRRING UP YOUR PROPHETIC GIFT

"Your spiritual gifts are already inside of you and when the Bible says "stir them up," it doesn't mean, beg, fast, or plead with God. Rather, it's an instruction to plug in and start operating! After all, you don't ask for what you have already; you use what you have already received."
(Emma Stark)

There have been occasions when I haven't posted a fresh word on my Daily Prophetic Instagram page for a few weeks. Invariably I have received several messages from kind and concerned people asking me if I'm okay? My reply is generally: "I'm fine thank you so much for asking. God just hasn't said anything to me."

While there are definite ebbs and flows in the amount of prophetic revelation we receive, I've also come to realize that often it's not a lack of communication on God's part – it's simply that I'm not positioned to receive what He might be saying. I'm too busy or pre-occupied to tune into the whisper from Heaven. On the other hand, when I take time to posture my heart in submission and surrender before the Lord, His voice becomes much more frequent and clear.

STOKE THE FLAMES

The Apostle Paul wrote this to his spiritual son:
"…I remind you to kindle afresh the gift of God which is in you through the laying on of my hands" (2 Timothy 1:6)

Other translations say:
"…stir up the gift of God…"
"…fan the flame of God's gift…"
"…keep ablaze the gift of God…"
"…stir up that inner fire which God gave you…"

A spiritual gift had been imparted to Timothy when Paul laid hands on him. It was now Timothy's responsibility to stir it up and develop it. Like any fire, if it wasn't attended to regularly, the flames would grow smaller and eventually die.

Similarly, each of us is called to stir up the gifts that God has placed within us. This includes the prophetic gift that I believe every Christian is graced with to varying degrees. Lack of attention will cause it to flounder and fade whereas fanning the flames will stoke it and stir it up to its full potential.

How do we do that?

Personally, I have found a number of spiritual practices and habits to be very effective in positioning me to hear God with increased regularity and clarity.

WORSHIP AND PRAYER

James 4: 8 says, "Draw near to God and he will draw near to you." God also told Jeremiah, "Call to me and I will
answer you and tell you great and unsearchable things you do not know.'

Spending significant time in God's presence, both in worship and prayer, 'activates' me to hear His voice. This can be personal or corporate. In church worship settings, often I will stop singing for a while and simply listen to what the Spirit is saying.

Wherever it is, the principle is the same – when you pursue and press into His presence, God will speak to you.

PRAY IN THE SPIRIT

Jude 1: 20 says: "But you, dear friends, by building yourselves up in your most holy faith and praying in the Holy Spirit…"

I'm aware that not every person reading this prays in tongues. That is a subject for another book. However, many believers who *can* pray in tongues, *don't*. Or if they do, it is sporadic and minimal.

I believe that praying in tongues is one of the most powerful things you can do to feed your spirit, increase your spiritual sensitivity, and stir up your gifts. In fact, in my experience, tongues is often the gift that activates all of the other gifts. Kathy DeGraw puts it like this:

"When we pray in tongues, our mind and thinking shut down, and we are praying and connecting our spirit man to the Holy Spirit. As we make that connection and our mind isn't analyzing, we can effectively hear from the Spirit of God and what He is calling us to release."

The great thing is that you can pray in tongues as you're driving, cooking, working and walking. Especially with hands-free being so prevalent today, people no longer think you're crazy when they see you talking to yourself!

At times, God may also give you the ability to interpret your prayer language. Or, as you're praying in tongues, you will receive visions and impressions.

Very often, when I pray in the Spirit, I keep a pen in my hand and a journal open because I am so expectant that God will speak. You should try that. Don't overthink what you sense or see. Just write it down as it comes into your mind.

LISTEN TO PROVEN PROPHETS

I find it very helpful to listen to teaching and prophetic revelations from trusted prophetic voices. These include Cindy Jacobs, Jane Hamon, Bill Hamon, Kris Vallotton, Bill Johnson, Sharon Stone, Julian Adams, and Emma Stark.

Often, something they say will spark a significant word within me. It's not that I'm copying them. It's simply that I'm being inspired by what God is saying through them. The Holy Spirit may emphasize one word or point that wasn't even central to their message.

It's also helpful to listen to and learn from *how* they share particular words. The tone, language, expressions and style can help you develop your own way of communicating what God shows you.

ASSOCIATION AND IMPARTATION

Seek out and begin to associate with proven prophetic people. You may well find that the anointing of God in them will 'rub off' on you. We see an example of this in 1 Samuel 19:20-21:

"Then Saul sent messengers to take David. And when they saw the group of prophets prophesying, and Samuel standing as leader over them, the Spirit of God came upon the messengers of Saul, and they also prophesied. And when Saul was told, he sent other messengers, and they prophesied likewise."

I love spending time around people who are further along in the prophetic than I am. It not only inspires me to press on and grow in my gift, but I also take every opportunity to have them lay hands on me and impart whatever the Lord wants to give me. One particular meeting with Randy Clark from *Global Awakening* comes to mind. It was at Holy Trinity Brompton in London. I'm not typically a 'faller', but when Randy laid hands on me, I flew into the air and landed on my back. When I eventually got to my feet, I immediately turned to some strangers around me and began to prophesy over them with an accuracy I'd never experienced up until that point. In fact, following this encounter in 2014, I began to notice a significant increase in my ability to hear from God and share what He was saying.

STAY CLEAN

Jesus said, "Blessed are the pure in heart, for they will see God." (Matthew 5: 8)

While we don't need to be perfect for our Father to speak to us, habitual sin will block or distort our interaction with Heaven. It will also affect our ability to clearly share what God says to others. As I said in an earlier chapter, we are a channel or conduit through which God speaks. If the pipe is dirty, anything that flows through it will also be tainted and polluted.

Keep short accounts with God. Don't permit sinful habits or unrepented sin to come between you and your intimacy with Christ.

BE EXPECTANT

Psalm 130: 6 says:
"I wait for the Lord
more than watchmen wait for the morning,
more than watchmen wait for the morning."

Watchmen are certain that the daylight will come so they wait with complete and confident expectation. Similarly, you too should have confidence that God wants to speak to you today.
Your expectation is God's invitation. When you live each moment with a sense of anticipation that God will speak, you are more likely to recognize His voice and respond quickly.

Remember, it is your birthright as a child of God to hear your Heavenly Father speak. Every day, everywhere, be attentive to what He might be saying.

When you go through a season when God doesn't seem to be speaking as often or as clearly, don't panic. We've all been there. You haven't 'lost it'. Keep pressing in and pursuing Him. I love what Helen Calder says: "Becoming aware of your spiritual dryness, and that you are finding it difficult to hear from God, is an indication that the Holy Spirit is drawing you to receive more from Him."

Practical Exercise:

If you pray in tongues, commit to spending a set amount of time each day for the next 30 days using your prayer language. Do what works for you: 5 minutes, 15 minutes, 30 minutes. As you pray, sit (or kneel) with a notebook and pen and scribble down any thoughts that come into your mind.

If you don't pray in tongues, repeat the above exercise using instrumental worship. You can find it easily on YouTube. As you listen for a set amount of time each day, expect God to speak and write it down.

DAY 30

IT'S TIME TO SPEAK OUT

"Spiritual gifts are empowerments provided by God to manifest His Kingdom and to rescue others. You have been weaponized by Heaven. You have remarkable ability, explosive strength, and forceful power!"
(Emma Stark)

As I write this final chapter, the United States is waiting to find out who their next President will be. It is a tense and tumultuous process with allegations of voter fraud and other polling violations. Whatever the election result, the coming days will likely bring more chaos and disorder to an already deeply fractured nation. All of this is coming at the end of 2020, a year that has turned life upside down with so much turmoil and upheaval.

What are we to do?

Where do we turn to find hope?

How do we avoid slipping into despondency and even despair?

We MUST hear the voice of God. Yes, through significant, proven prophetic voices. But also daily in our personal lives. It is imperative that we lean into the Father's heart and listen to what He is saying. Discerning the mind of God is the only way to find strength and stability in a world that is being shaken and reshaped in ways unimaginable just 12 months ago.

It's interesting to note that all of the major prophetic books in the Bible were written during times of crisis for God's people. Isaiah, Jeremiah, Ezekiel, Daniel, and others, show us that God is not inattentive or unconcerned about what is going on in our lives and world right now. In fact, in seasons of turbulence and disruption, God communicates with greater clarity and frequency. He shows His people the way forward through the mayhem and confusion. His voice reminds us of our identity and points us towards our destiny.

BE A VOICE, NOT AN ECHO

Today, God wants to speak to you and God wants to speak through you. Hopefully you are grasping that by now. The Father loves to communicate His heart, His plans, and His purposes to His people.

However, He is not simply looking for a voice – He wants to speak through *your* voice. You are not a copy or a clone. God gave you your unique personality, quirks, and idiosyncrasies. He created your DNA and implanted your deepest desires. He wired you to love and loathe certain things. And He wants to use all of that to express His heart for the world around you. So, don't hide your light or try to be anyone else. Shine brightly, speak passionately, live courageously, love extravagantly.

I have always hated the sound of my own voice. I would cringe when I heard recordings of me speaking or preaching. I even seriously considered going for voice classes to change it to something more appealing to the ear. Then, not long ago, I took my little boy to a new barbershop in town. The owner and staff all happened to be believers. As soon as I spoke, they said, "You're Craig Cooney. We listen to you online every week. We were just saying the other day how much we love your voice." I was genuinely stunned. I even tipped them double for their kind words!

At around the same time, an audio clip of me challenging a local politician ended up being played on the biggest morning talk show in the country. Even though I was never named, everyone knew it was me because, apparently, my voice is so distinctive.

I began to realize that one of my personal features that I most disliked was actually something that God was using to make an impact. While I still don't love hearing myself on recordings, I have definitely become more free and confident in expressing my voice. If God has given me something to say, I need to be uninhibited in expressing it.

It's the same with you. God will take all that you are, even the parts you might not especially like, and use them for His glory. Your unique voice will resonate with certain people that others would struggle to connect with. Or as I heard someone say recently, "your vibe will attract your tribe". It's true. When you show up authentic and real, even with your blemishes and imperfections on display, people will be drawn to you and you can then point them to God.

The reality is, sometimes God will give you a prophetic word or message that may not be especially popular or politically correct. You could lose friends and followers if you share it. The temptation will be to stay silent or tone it down. However, if you don't express it, you will shut down something within yourself. You will become increasingly controlled by fear and the opinions of others. Your life will shrink and your light will be dimmed.

Speak whatever God tells you to say, even if it's uncomfortable or unpopular. Communicate it with love and compassion, but also with a holy boldness and deep conviction. The world needs His Word.

IT'S YOUR TIME

The famous preacher A.W. Tozer once said, "A scared world needs a fearless church." How true that is for the times we are currently living in. God's people must not succumb to the pandemic of fear and anxiety which surrounds us. The Word of God calls us to demonstrate boldness and courage as well as compassion and kindness. If God is really on His throne, ruling with complete supremacy and unrivaled authority, what do we have to be afraid of?

As a prophetic people, we are the tellers of truth, upholders of righteousness, and makers of history. We will not be muzzled by the world or silenced by the enemy. We are more concerned with being prophetically direct than politically correct. We stand for justice, kneel in humility, pray with authority, and walk in holiness. We will not cower to the culture or be intimidated by those who shout the loudest. We will continually advance, take new ground, and extend the rule of God's Kingdom into every place and space.

These are perilous and precarious days. Truly we have not been this way before. We simply cannot settle for 'business as usual' in the Body of Christ. The power of God *must* be seen. The voice of God *must* be heard. The heart of God *must* be expressed. This *must* happen through *you*.

It is time to break agreement with small thinking and shrunken living. The Lord is on the move and we cannot settle for 'same-old'. Prepare to receive downloads from Heaven of wisdom and revelation for this hour. Expect to experience the manifest and tangible presence of God as a daily reality. Believe that the best is yet to come and that you will walk in a greater anointing than you could ever imagine. Anticipate that you will hear the Father's voice with an increased clarity and frequency than ever before. Look forward to a release of prosperity and provision to fulfill the plans and purposes of God in this season of great shifting and shaking. Get ready for the glory of the Lord to cover the earth as the waters cover the sea (Habakkuk 2: 14).

You were born for such a time as this.

All of the resources of Heaven are available to you.

Open your mouth and speak.

Mountains will move. Dead things will come to life. Barrenness will be broken. Darkness will be illuminated. Diseases will be healed. Captives will be set free.

The Word of the Lord is inside you. Let it out.

Printed in Great Britain
by Amazon